JESUS in Two Perspectives

JESUS in Two Perspectives

A Jewish–Christian Dialog

Pinchas Lapide
& Ulrich Luz

Translated by Lawrence W. Denef

AUGSBURG Publishing House • Minneapolis

JESUS IN TWO PERSPECTIVES
A Jewish-Christian Dialog

Library of Congress Cataloging-in-Publication Data

Lapide, Pinchas, 1922-
JESUS IN TWO PERSPECTIVES.

Translation of: Der Jude Jesus.
Bibliography: p.
1. Jesus Christ—Jewish interpretations. I. Luz, Ulrich. II. Title.
BM620.L35513 1985 232 85-15760
ISBN 0-8066-2171-0

Manufactured in the U.S.A. APH 10-3517

1 2 3 4 5 6 7 8 9 0 1 2 3 4 5 6 7 8 9

Contents

Part One: A Jewish Perspective *by Pinchas Lapide*

Introduction 9

Thesis One: Jesus did not declare himself to his people as Messiah 27

Thesis Two: The people of Israel did not reject Jesus 57

Thesis Three: Jesus never repudiated his people 85

Prolog for tomorrow 111

Part Two: A Christian Perspective *by Ulrich Luz*

Introduction 123

Response to Thesis One 129

Response to Thesis Two 139

Response to Thesis Three 149

Concerning the dialog for tomorrow 157

Notes 167

Part One

A Jewish Perspective

by Pinchas Lapide

Introduction

Narrowmindedness can cause those who believe differently to be calumniated as unbelievers, and often even to be demonized as subhumans. That is the sorry result of almost 2000 years of separation between Jews and Christians. Over the centuries the arrogance of such theological apartheid apparently caused little concern. Only in our day has the biblical truth dawned upon us that the universal fatherhood of God inevitably places all believers under one and the same limitless and loving grace. This grace knows of no hopelessly lost stepchildren nor does it acknowledge the special salvation of a select few.

Thanks to this insight we today stand at the threshold of a previously unimaginable dialog, the first impartial conversation about faith between the actual living brothers of Jesus and his spiritual disciples—since church and synagogue parted ways. Two things must be taken to heart, lest old claims to absolute truth become a stumbling block, and in order to ensure that this dialog is carried on vertically—that is, before

God and under God, without degenerating into a horizontal controversy between the opinionated and the prejudiced.

First, all of us, whether we gather in houses of worship that bear the star of David or the cross, know next to nothing about the first and the last things. We *believe* with the firmest conviction of our hearts, but none of us can logically demonstrate the foundations of his or her religion. This should instill in all of us that essential humility which ought to characterize every proper faith conversation. True dialog must be based on complete frankness which leads to no giddy deception of artificial fellowship such as Martin Buber warned against, but rather which clarifies and discusses everything that lies on our hearts. So let us be honest, even if it is not without pain.

When it is a matter of a global overview of Christian-Jewish relationships every Jew is a Jeremiah in whose heart "there is . . . as it were a burning fire shut up in my bones, and I am weary with holding it in, and I cannot" (Jer. 20:9).

The following pages are not so much concerned with accusation and denunciation as they are with overcoming a traumatic past that continues to poison the present and overshadow every dialog with its horrifying memories. Here the words of Job apply, "I must speak, that I may find relief; I must open my lips and answer" (Job 32:20), in order to give voice to that which has too long remained unsaid and been shrouded in deadly silence. So then, you Christians, listen to that which troubles my heart! "Consider, and then we will speak" (Job 18:2).

"See how many charges they bring against you" (Mark 15:4). For 1900 years this statement of Pilate has applied to the people of Israel, still standing before the judgment seat, forced to endure a flood of slanderous reproaches: "You Jews crucified the Savior!" At first we attempted to reply, "Crucifixion is a

Roman means of execution. Under their rule we weren't even allowed to impose the death sentence." Then we appealed to the New Testament, "But that isn't what the Gospels say!" Yet what help are facts when fanaticism is at play? "Is it not Jesus whom we have slandered, spit upon, beaten, and eventually crucified?" The Epistle of Barnabas (7:9), written about A.D. 125, places these words into the mouth of a fictitious "Jew," in order to fabricate a confession which never crossed the lips of any Jew.

The crime was so outrageous and despicable that the church fathers coined a new term to describe it: deicide. Every Jewish pen instinctively recoils at the translation of this blasphemy: the murder of God. No wonder that the slaying of such "Christ killers" was soon elevated to a God-pleasing deed. In the language of the Inquisition, burning Jews alive became an "act of faith." Naturally, for those who could lay hands on the Savior, crimes such as the poisoning of wells, ritual murder, the desecration of sacraments, spreading the plague, the poisoning of children, the Judas kiss, and the casting of spells on Christians were but minor infractions.

From the long list of church fathers who fanned the flames of prejudice it is enough to mention Chrysostom (354–407) who called the synagogue "a brothel, a den of spiritual iniquity, and the abode of Satan," and concluded his almost endless catalog of Jewish vices with the three words that eventually came to characterize the Jews in medieval Christendom: "God hates you!" (*Adv. Jud.* 1:3; 1:7; 6:6; 7:1).

The murder-and-curse theories of certain theologians, which were later taken up by the Reformation, spared no rhetorical or artistic means to translate this alleged "hatred of God" into an effective form of human hatred. The Ten Commandments, the Sermon on the Mount, the commission to love one's enemies, indeed, the entire ethic of the Nazarene lost their validity for those who selfishly believed they had a monopoly on God's love. "Truly, I say to you, as you did it to one of the least of these my brethren, you did it to me" (Matt. 25:40). Jesus was crucified afresh a thousand times by nominal Christians who made his brothers the scum of the earth.

No less than 96 church councils and 114 popes issued edicts against the Jews, mocking, scorning, disinheriting, and dispossessing them, treating them as pariahs, and bringing Israel to the brink of destruction. "The mass murder of Jews by the Nazis was the work of godless criminals," writes Hans Küng, "but without the almost 2000-year history of 'Christian' anti-Judaism . . . it would have been impossible. . . . None of the anti-Jewish measures taken by the Nazis—marked clothing, exclusion from various occupations, the prohibition of mixed marriages, plundering, expulsion, concentration camps, outright slaughter, and cremation—was new. All of these were already a part of medieval Christendom."[1] "Christians have always perpetrated the gravest, most appalling atrocities against the Jews," writes Karl Rahner. "We must face up to this charge; we must allow the plaintiffs who tell us what Christians have done to the Jews free reign to speak."[2]

"Why do you persecute me?" is the unanswered question of the Risen One (Acts 22:7) and of millions of his brothers who have repeatedly been nailed to the cross of anti-Judaism.

In vain Bernard of Clairvaux preached to the leaders of the first crusades: "Go to Zion, protect the grave of Christ your Lord, but do not harm the sons of Israel . . . for they are the flesh and bone of the Messiah, and if you molest them you run the risk of injuring the apple of God's eye!" His warnings fell on deaf ears.

"Baptism or death" was the cry of the crusaders as they

assaulted the Jewish communities of the Rhineland. And when the Jews remained true to their faith they were cut down on the spot with cross-swords "in the name of Jesus Christ." In the hands of Christians the crucifix again became the instrument of death it had once been in pagan hands.

The man of Nazareth was right when he said to his followers, "You will be hated by all for my name's sake" (Mark 13:13). An uninterrupted way of the cross begins at Golgotha, an unspeakably sorrowful passion story of blood and tears that finds its end in Auschwitz. Throughout it all the gospel was lost. Brutality and lust for power gained the upper hand and the Jews became the victims.

If humility, resolute faith, trust in God, and the silent endurance of persecution belong to the heart of the Christian life, then the Jews were the most faithful followers of their great brother from Nazareth. Such is the opinion of the Protestant theologian Helmut Gollwitzer: "If anyone has been a community of the cross during these centuries, it is the Jews, who were so often struck down by the community of the crucified, and who have, in a unique way, more than the victorious church, become the cross-bearers of history. The cross of God's election lies upon them; we have adorned ourselves with the cross long enough, without bearing it."[3] The end result: never have so many hated so few for so long without reason.

"You have rejected the Lord Christ!" This became the pretext for the most malicious inhumanities ever perpetrated in the name of a religion of love. "Have *you* actually accepted him?" would be a legitimate Jewish response.

"Why do you call me 'Lord, Lord,' and not do what I tell you?" (Luke 6:46) was the reproach of the Man who called for discipleship rather than adoration. Do you love your enemies? Do you pray for those who persecute you? Have you ever turned the other cheek? Do you seek reconciliation with your Jewish brothers and sisters? Do you forgive those who trespass against you in order that you might be forgiven? When those who are last finally become the first, where will you be? Are you so guiltless that you dare to throw stones at us?

For many Christians the fact that a sanctified remnant of Israel was able to survive the flood of butchery, persecution, and mass murder later became the best proof for the existence of God. Already around 1140 Peter Abelard wrote, "We would declare God to be cruel if we thought the steadfastness of the Jews under tribulation could remain without reward. No nation has suffered so much for God."[4] For the maltreated, outcast people, driven from one horror to another, the cross became the epitome of maliciousness—and Jesus, who personified the hatred they experienced, their archenemy.

Still the church could not manage without the synagogue. From the very beginning a remarkable ambivalence, apparently an eternal bond, characterized the relationship between Jesus' brothers and his disciples.

Jesus, Mary, and the initial founders of the church all emerged from the people of Israel. Yet it is "the Jews," according to John's Gospel, who put Jesus on the cross and, even worse for many teachers of the church, they have to this very day refused to recognize the Savior of the world in their "brother according to the flesh." Jesus announced that he "was sent only to the lost sheep of the house of Israel" (Matt. 15:24), yet the Resurrected One commissioned his disciples to baptize "all nations" (Matt. 28:19). Without Jesus there would be no Christians, though he himself remained a Jew throughout his life.

"Salvation is from the Jews," according to the Gospel of John (4:22). But shortly thereafter the Jews are told, "You are of your father the devil" (John 8:44). Matthew declares them incurably stubborn (Matt. 13:10-15), in order that they might be disinherited by the Gentile church (Matt. 21:43)—whereas Paul sees Christendom merely as a new branch that has by grace been grafted into the tree of Israel (Rom. 11:16ff.).

No wonder that these and other contradictions have led to a profound ambiguity in the Christian position. On the one hand there is a sense of affirmation. Already in the second century there was a platonic love for abstract Israel, the "people of the Bible," since both Testaments were written mainly by Jews, about Jews, and primarily for Jews. Moreover, they were written for the people of the "old covenant," inasmuch as all the covenants of the Hebrew Bible are intended for the corporeal people of Israel. And they were written for the "brothers of Jesus according to the flesh," inasmuch as the reality of Jesus' Jewishness could not be suppressed in any of the New Testament writings.

On the other hand a growing enmity developed toward the "perfidious Jews," because they had remained true to their faith throughout 3000 years; to the "treacherous Jews," because a certain Judas had allegedly betrayed his Lord for 30 pieces of silver; and finally to the "Christ-killers," because the Fourth Gospel attributes the principal blame for Jesus' death to his own brothers in faith.

The two halves of this love-hate relationship were, however, by no means balanced. While love assumed the form of an ethereal myth, the tangible expression of which was confined to religious art, the Jews of Europe became the living target of hatred. They—as Pope Innocent IV in a Bull of 1247 affirmed with great satisfaction—"now find themselves under a more grievous rule than their fathers experienced under Pharaoh in Egypt."

The Christian view of suffering, which has over the centuries undergone no significant change, is also strongly ambivalent. The passion of Jesus, with all of its excruciating horror, is immortalized in words and pictures, in stone, glass, and wood, as the most sublime demonstration of God's gracious love. Yet the sufferings of the Jews, from Roman crucifixions, through the torture chambers and burnings of the dark ages to the gas chambers of our day, are either suppressed or regarded, consciously or unconsciously, as evidences of "divine rejection." "Blessed are those who are persecuted for righteousness' sake, for theirs is the kingdom of heaven" (Matt. 5:10). Does not this word of Jesus, addressed to his brothers, regard suffering as a sign that weakness and powerlessness can become means of grace?

"You Jews suffer," gloated Justin more than 1800 years ago. "Your country is a wasteland; Jerusalem lies destroyed, for you have killed the Savior!" (Dialogue with Trypho 16). This malicious joy concerning the sufferings of Jesus' brothers, so flagrantly expressed in innumerable formulations, has—with the concerted efforts of Christians—become the indispensable shadow side of the Christian view of salvation history. Apparently the love of Jesus can find its fullest expression only when it is accompanied and amplified by hatred for the Jews. It is a basic principle of drama that in order for the hero of a play to make his greatest impact there must always be a villain. Does the religion of love also require an eternal villain as a scapegoat in order to get rid of its hatred for unbelievers and in order to accentuate the light of Jesus against the dark backdrop of "the Jews"?

We hope that the shadow side of fanaticism lies behind us. Absolutism, conformity, and the tendency to think in terms of black-and-white are slowly giving way to new attitudes.

Christians have reluctantly but noticeably begun the task of eliminating such antibiblical pseudotheologies as "the murder of God," those Judas legends that portray the betrayer as a symbol of the entire people, and the Ahasuerus legend of the Jews eternally cursed as wanderers.

There is ferment and unrest in all churches. Roman and Greek thought patterns and religious forms so foreign to our modern ways are crumbling. Everywhere teachings are being revised, doctrines reexamined, and old formulations restated in order to open a way to the essential faith of the Nazarene who lived and died on behalf of his people Israel.

The Protestant theologian Jürgen Moltmann calls this new wave of enthusiasm "the Hebrew wave" because of its passion for the church's rediscovery of Judaism and because of its insistence that "one cannot read the New Testament without the Old Testament. Only beside each other and with each other do they disclose the fullness of life in faith. Moreover, one soon discovers that Jesus of Nazareth is not merely the wall that separates Christians from Jews, but above all else the bridge between them."[5]

We have finally reached that point. Providence has freed the churches from the temptation to use secular power and helped the Jews, through their newly established sovereignty, to achieve a modest sense of self-confidence that does not have to depend solely upon tactical considerations. At last we can speak freely and openly with one another. In previous Christian-Jewish conversations, when they did occur, the separate roles were strictly adhered to. Christians took the religious "offensive"; they determined the themes, fixed the agenda, set the tone of every double monolog, and staged disputation and compulsory conversation. Jews, on the other hand, remained on the defensive, polemical one moment, apologetic the next, but always limited to saying *no*: no to Christology, no to the resurrection, and a capital NO to Paul.

Today triumphal omnipotence no longer characterizes the churches, nor secular impotence the Jews. As a result, coercion by a majority and the fear of reprisal no longer curtail freedom of speech; thus an honest exchange of opinions is possible.

"The church dare not conduct itself as if it were speaking to one who is ignorant," says the study *Israel and the Church,* published on behalf of the General Synod of the Dutch Reformed Church.[6] "Such talk is rejected by the Jewish people, and rightly so. It is befitting that a younger sister converse with an older brother . . . but in order for the conversation to be mutually satisfying she must be willing to listen." So today there are several reasons for Jews actively to contribute to the reevaluation of thought taking place within the churches.

Of primary concern is the fundamental lack of symmetry between the two faiths. The church, from its very beginnings, has been interested in those principal questions regarding faith, transcendental ideology, and the truths of salvation which are customarily incorporated into theological systems. The Jews, on the other hand, have very little theology in the Christian sense of this Greek word. Instead, their faith is grounded in a revealed way of life that makes daily deeds of faith, rather than faith itself, the true test of divine approval.

Jesus was a Jew and as such he was not a theologian. He did his best to provide practical, though at times radical, answers to very human problems. His teachings, even when they were idealistic expressions of discontent, never left the plane of earthly reality. Only later did his followers, who were then by and large no longer Jews, attempt to squeeze him along with his easily remembered paradoxes into a logical straitjacket. And he is still protesting, "I am no cleverly-thought-out book; I am a human being, with all the inherent contradictions."

Regarding Jewish "non-theology," which tries to avoid translating God's saving actions into scientific abstractions, Pastor Martin Stöhr says: "Is not the Jewish way of doing theology—with its constant questioning and counterquestioning, its emphasis on the whole, its inclusion of contradictory traditions, its rejection of schematization, and its willingness to forego seeing Holy Scriptures as a unity or finding in them some 'material principle'—more appropriate to the historicity of divine revelation than the Christian dogmatic tradition?"[7]

Be that as it may, Jews must appear to most Christians as doubting Thomases who are always concerned with tangible realities, even in matters relating to faith. This, however, coincides with the lesson given to Moses for our instruction when he sought to see God's face: "You cannot see my face; for man shall not see me and live"—such was the Creator's reply (Exod. 33:20). The words that follow indicate that at the very most Moses would be allowed to see God's "back." From then on we Jews have contented ourselves with seeing things from behind, that is, after they have occurred. For our sages this has meant the probing of God's saving activity in retrospect, an approach which often makes it possible to discern the evidence of God's otherwise unfathomable will.

Precisely this retrospective approach today enables us to look at Jesus anew and reassess his significance in the light of his worldwide impact. By comparison, Christian theologians remind many Jews of the "men of Galilee" who, as the book of Acts reports, stood "gazing into heaven" until they were rebuked by two angels, "Why do you stand looking into heaven?" (Acts 1:10f.). Isn't there enough here on earth to gaze at, to explore, and to do? This interest in heaven, it seems, inevitably leads to a theology which victimized the Jews—not theologically or scholastically, but historically, bodily, and actually. How did it happen?

Christianity emerged from a messianic faction within Judaism that provided it with all its fundamental principles and initial impulses. "The church as a whole," writes Karl Barth, "still owes everything to those to whom it is indebted for everything [the Jews]."[8] Gradually, often painfully, the Christian movement detached itself from its mother faith and established its independent identity as church. But no sooner did the young religion leave the homeland of its founder to attend school in Greece, than a new "Judaism" was given birth, primarily in the writings of the church fathers, its cerebral existence largely determined by their otherworldly abstractions. Apart from the name *Judaism*, it had very little in common with the real Jewish people.

Nevertheless, it was the actual Jewish people who suffered as a whipping boy for the sins attributed to this "Judaism"—a fictitious caricature of a pseudo-Israel shaped to fit the new worldview of the predominantly Gentile church. This was a purely intellectual construct that could afford the luxury of ignoring all the conflicting historical facts because it was supposedly based on the knowledge of salvation as well as on the discernment of God's will. The purpose of this fantasy was to resolve a basic dilemma of the early church, a dilemma that still plagues many Christian theologians—Jewish "unbelief." The "solution" is so simple that it can be stated in a single sentence: Since Jesus lived his entire life as a Jew among Jews and for Jews, and the Jews do not accept him as their Savior, they must be spiritually blind or diabolically malicious, or perhaps both. Since all other answers appeared to shake the very foundations of the Christian gospel, this pat answer was already fostered with diligence and imagination before the end of the first century. Ever more clearly, Jesus, in the writings of the church, was transformed into the Messiah of Israel; ever more abrupt his rejection by "the Jews" seemed; and ever more shrill Jesus' condemnation of Israel sounded. As Christology evolved, each new exaltation of the Nazarene seemed logically to necessitate a further humiliation of his people. And so, within a few decades the hallowed people of God could become the "synagogue of Satan" whose sole purpose it was to endure the curse of God and through their misery, as Pope Innocent III proclaimed, "bear witness to the truth of Christendom."[9]

That this primitive anti-Judaism of the thoughtless Gentile world has, to this very day, been allowed to impose its narrowminded scheme of black-and-white on the entire history of salvation is a scandal, in the face of which all other problems of Jewish-Christian relationships pale into insignificance. "Enmity against the Jewish people is still based on the assumption that they continue to bear the unpardoned guilt for rejecting and crucifying God's Son, the Savior of the world, and that as a result of this religious offense they will remain the sons of Satan until they repent." So wrote the Catholic author and historian Karl Thieme in 1963.[10] The Protestant theologian Johann Maier reaffirmed this view in 1976: "That which in our day still characterizes the Christian image of Judaism is not actual knowledge of the religious history of Judaism, but rather . . . a Christian theology of Judaism which is often based on untenable assertions and prejudices."[11]

In her anthology of misconceptions about Judaism, Charlotte Klein documents how untenable—a whole generation after Auschwitz—their assertions really are. Many of her citations are from the most famous pens in contemporary theology. A few representative excerpts should serve to illustrate the trend:[12]

> Jesus is the Messiah promised by the Old Testament, but the chosen people rejected him and this resulted in the rejection of the nation in salvation history (but not eternally).
>
> (Günther Schiwy, *Weg ins NT,* vol. 1 [Würzburg, 1970], p. 162; cited by Klein, p. 99.)

> The curse will accompany this people—reduced to a remnant—throughout history, and will call down one judgment after another on them, but one day it will come to an end.
>
> (Michael Schmaus, *Katholische Dogmatik,* vol. 4.2 [Munich, 1963], p. 168; cited by Klein, p. 108.)

> Israel has "fallen". . . . It is lying on the ground. . . . There is a cover over the rigid Torah and there is a cover over their hard hearts. . . . They do not perceive how blindness becomes "hardening" or "obstinacy" on the part of the individual.
>
> (Heinrich Schlier, *Die Zeit der Kirche* [Freiburg, 1972], p. 241; cited by Klein, p. 109.)

> Jesus' message remained within the framework of Judaism. Yet it was this Judaism that gave rise to the enmity that led to his death. Moreover, by calling for his death Judaism determined its own destiny. It was not the military campaigns of Rome but animosity toward Christians that led to continued exile.
>
> (Martin Dibelius, *Botschaft und Geschichte* [Tübingen, 1953], p. 103.

> They rejected Jesus Christ. . . . By rejecting Christ they abandoned their own history, the basis of their existence as God's people. That is the reason why they themselves are rejected.
> (M. Schmaus, *Katholische Dogmatik,* vol. 3.1, p. 79; cited by Klein, p. 107.)

Concerning Charlotte Klein's "well-ordered collection of anti-Judaica," David Flusser of Jerusalem says, "Has anyone ever considered that such words and similar utterances are punishable offenses; that they . . . provoke homicide?" *(Freiburg Newsletter* 27 [1975]: 139).

As long as "the Jews" are still widely "judged," "rejected," "damned," and "cursed" in dozens of authoritative textbooks, no Christian-Jewish dialog that does not first concern itself with the eradication of these remaining non-Christian teachings of hatred can be taken seriously.

We want to be frank with our Christian colleagues who, like us, are struggling for greater biblical ecumenism. When one takes into account the friendliness, the courteousness, the sense of guilt, and the praiseworthy expressions of humanity in most of the church statements about the Jews made since the second World War, one must, on the one hand, conclude that Jews are to be respected as persons, that one ought to come to their aid when their human rights are threatened, indeed, that seeking to understand them is worth the effort. On the other hand, one gets the impression that Judaism as a religion does not really need to be discussed since, from the perspective of church doctrine, Judaism does not exist as a valid way of salvation.

Even after a quarter century of dialog there is no catholic *Tractatus de judaeis,* nor is there a Protestant theology of Israel which is in a position to express the spirit of Jesus and constructively replace the old teachings of contempt and hatred.

Naturally this cannot happen overnight. To reshape thought forms that have developed over thousands of years requires no less than the renewal of preaching and exegesis, but especially of theology.

Some Jews might well respond, "None of these things is of concern to us; they are internal affairs of the church." Questions such as the understanding of the Eucharist, the office of ministry, and the Trinity may well be internal matters for the church; but a reconsideration of the church's attitude toward Jews and Judaism is for us a matter of life and death. For all too long we have been the silent, passive objects of a church theology whose myth about the "murder of God" eventually led to the actual murder of millions of Jews. "Deicide" fathered genocide.

Christians on the other hand might ask, "What have Jews to do with Christian theology?" Inasmuch as Christian Old Testament scholars have for hundreds of years engaged in exploring the Hebrew Bible, it is only right that Jewish New Testament scholars be involved in today's quest for the earthly Jesus and his message—all the more since, as we have learned from experience, the influence of Christian theologies will surely have a direct effect on future generations of Jews.

As the first step on this long journey we must correct three errors that have served as the roots of that ancient "Christian" animosity for the Jews: Jesus was the Messiah of Israel; Jesus was rejected by the Jews; Jesus has in turn repudiated them.

In the following pages we are not interested in syncretism, or in developing a Jewish antithesis to the church's teachings, and certainly not with the reputation of Christian truths. To eliminate antiscriptural hostility and to undergird biblical love for one's neighbor is the sole intention of the author.

If it should be proved, on the basis of the New Testament accounts:

- that Jesus never revealed himself to his people as their Messiah;
- that Israel therefore could not accept him as their redeemer;
- that the majority of Jews whom Jesus addressed gave him an enthusiastic reception;
- that it is impossible to speak of "Jewish guilt" in connection with the crucifixion;
- that even as Jesus never rejected his people, Israel never rejected Jesus; and
- that Jesus' undivided love for his people continues to be valid even beyond his death;

then Christian theology could not silently skirt these facts. It would have to examine them seriously, in order to ascertain the extent to which they would necessitate a new interpretation of the Jewish rejection of Christology after Jesus, as well as a reevaluation of its own theological position regarding Judaism. It is to such a reconsideration, which could well provide a breakthrough in the dialog between Jesus' disciples and his brothers, that this book is dedicated.

It is the author's chief purpose to provide theological building blocks for the construction of a biblical bridge. But whether or not the bridge can be built remains an open question. Nineteen hundred years without dialog have generated colossal mounds of mutual mistrust and polemical debris that block almost every theological access. This book must be understood as an attempt to clear away the debris that has for so long hampered and inhibited communication. It aims to uncover that which has been buried and encrusted, especially the mutual recognition of Jews and Christians as closely related faith communities, who despite their admitted differences, live as brothers and sisters under the same Father-God, build upon his gracious love, pray for his succor, and earnestly hope for his salvation.

All New Testament passages quoted in the following chapters are treated primarily according to the history of their effect rather than from a historical-critical perspective.

Thesis One

Jesus did not declare himself to his people as Messiah

Dictionaries describe "the Messiah" primarily as "the promised deliverer of the Jews," who in time also becomes known as "the Redeemer of humankind," or more specifically as "the liberator of all oppressed peoples." As the anointed king and representative of God he embodies truth and righteousness and, on assuming power, will restore divine order to a world that has gone awry. The necessity of his coming reflects the prevailing realistic assessment of Judaism regarding the corruption of all political power. The certainty of his coming arises from the confidence Jews have in God's continuing care for his creation. The indestructible optimism of the Jewish people finds its source in their steadfast hope for the reappearance of spiritual reality in human history, to which the Messiah's advent will testify.

Viewed historically, messianism is a child of Jewish affliction and of an enduring Jewish faith which, despite every appearance, clings tenaciously to the ultimate victory of good over evil. When earthly rulers fail, the ancient longing for a restored world gives rise to the image of an ideal ruler, who at long last takes seriously the universal kingship of God, in order to reveal to everyone the supreme lordship of the Creator.

The Hebrew Bible at first views the Messiah solely as a king whose anointing by a prophet or high priest legitimates him for political rule under God. However, during times of national catastrophe and tribulation the understanding of Messiah changes. Expanded to include the tolerant Gentile emperor Cyrus (Isa. 45:1), the suffering servant of God (Isaiah 53), the king of the poor (Zech. 9:9), and one who comes from the clouds of heaven "like a son of man" (Dan. 7:13), the image of the Messiah is indirectly transformed into a saving lord whose task it is to spread the eschatological rule of peace from Jerusalem to the ends of the earth. The greater the misery of oppression, the more majestic the portrayal of the bringer of salvation becomes, and the more immediate and intense the expectation of his arrival. Consistent with Judaism's penchant for religious pluralism, a colorful variety of messianic hopes emerged under the pressure of the Roman yoke—though, for the most part, these hopes were concerned primarily with the kingdom of God which the Messiah as the obedient agent of God was to establish, rather than with the person of the Messiah himself.

Whether he would come as a restoration Messiah to reestablish the kingdom of David, or as a utopian Messiah to inaugurate Isaiah's vision of world peace, or as an apocalyptic Messiah, a zealot on "a white horse" clad "in a robe dipped in blood," with "a sharp sword" to "smite the nations," as the Revelation of St. John says (19:1-21), all of the various forms of messianic hope have one thing in common—the God-given political role of deliverance, which the coming one was to accomplish publicly on the stage of world history.

The role of the messianic kings of the Bible was political; all of the messianic prophecies concerning the last days were politically colored; the plight of Israel out of which the Messiah was to save God's people was primarily political. A nonpolitical Messiah would have been a self-contradiction during the rule of Rome. The spiritualizing of the salvation for which everyone longed—for instance, in the sense of saving an immaterial soul—would have been perceived as antibiblical escapism, indeed, as a denial of historical-political responsibility for this God-created world. In other words, it was anticipated from the fervently expected anointed of the Lord that "we should be saved from our enemies, and from the hand of all who hate us," so that "we, being delivered from the hand of our enemies, might serve him [God] without fear" (Luke 1:71ff.), as the aged Zechariah says in the *Benedictus,* or as Mary, following Hannah's footsteps (1 Sam. 2:1-10), reaffirms (Luke 1:51-55), and as the prophetess, Anna, the daughter of Phanuel, subsequently repeats in the temple when she "spoke of him to all who were looking for the redemption of Jerusalem" (Luke 2:38). Jesus of Nazareth did not fulfill any of these expectations—nor did he ever promise to fulfill them.

"I am the Messiah" (Matt. 24:5, author's translation). Matthew alone includes these words which could at the very least have clearly made Jesus a messianic pretender. But he allows Jesus to utter them just once, neither as a self-assertion nor as a declaration concerning his future office, but rather as a warning to his disciples to beware of false messiahs who would claim the title of savior as their own—a title which Jesus never expressly applied to himself.

Looking at the whole picture, this warning is actually a

decisive refutation of Jesus' alleged messianic self-consciousness. No one who is conscious of being called as the messianic redeemer of Israel needs to fear the later misuse of this honored title.

"Did Jesus reinterpret the traditional Messiah-concept?" asks Rudolf Bultmann, along with many others who, as a provisional solution, advocate Jesus' "spiritualization" of this title. Responding to his own question, Bultmann states, "Only the tradition could inform us as to that. But where in it is such a thing indicated? Where, in the words of Jesus, is there polemic against the conventional Messiah-concept? It is no more to be found than is any criticism of the Jewish conception of the Reign of God."[1]

The same holds true of miracle workers, several of whom are mentioned in early rabbinic literature. Their healings,[2] exorcisms,[3] stillings of storms,[4] multiplying of bread,[5] or raising of the dead[6] were never associated with messianism. On the other hand, Bar Kochba, the leader of a Jewish rebellion against Roman rule in the second century A.D. functioned for almost three years as a rabbinically authenticated "Messiah,"[7] without ever having performed a single miracle. In the case of "the suffering servant of God" (Isaiah 53) it has been established historically that "only later was Isaiah 53 associated with the Messiah."[8] "Actually the thought of a suffering Messiah was completely remote from the synagogue of Jesus' time."[9] To this fact R. Bultmann adds: "In addition, the tradition of Jesus' sayings reveals no trace of a consciousness on his part of being the Servant of God of Is. 53. . . . It is significant that Paul himself nowhere adduces the figure of the Servant of God."[10]

Insofar as the Messiah ben Joseph, the "dying Messiah," is concerned,[11] Martin Hengel and other scholars invariably report that belief in him first "arose after the middle of the second century."[12]

A Catholic theologian best summarizes the state of affairs regarding the resurrection and Easter appearances: "For Jewish scholars the evidence of the resurrection was not a proof of Jesus' messiahship, because for them the idea of resurrection was not connected with the messianic expectation of salvation. In Jesus' day, Judaism expected the reappearance of various figures . . . but not the resurrection of the Messiah."[13]

Jesus proved to be correct in his warning about false messiahs. In the very century after his crucifixion no less than six messianic claimants made an appearance. Though none of them was able to achieve any real deliverance, they all succeeded in leading thousands of credulous Jews to death or slavery.

Josephus, the Jewish historian of the first century A.D., reports (*Ant.* 20.97) that in the year 44, Theudas, the "prophet" and messianic pretender, managed to lead "a large number of his followers" to the Jordan River where his promise to part the waters of the Jordan as Joshua had done (Josh. 3:8ff.) proved futile.

In the year 53 the Roman governor, Antonius Felix, succeeded in outwitting, capturing, and deporting to Rome Eleasar ben Dineus, the "ringleader" of the messianic rebels, who had hoped to carry on the work of liberation begun by the sons of Judas the Galilean. In the year 66 in Jerusalem, Manachem, the commander of the zealots, a fanatical party within Judaism who were involved primarily in the Jewish insurrection of 67–70, encouraged his own veneration as Messiah and assumed the leadership of the rebel movement. Shortly thereafter he, along with others of them, was crucified by the Romans.

In the year 70, even though the entire city of Jerusalem was in Roman hands, Simon bar Giora, clothed in the robes of messianic royalty, made one last desperate attempt to force God's intervention. He was taken captive, led to Rome in a victory procession by Titus, and there publicly put to death along with other zealots.

Around the turn of the year 73-74, a sicarius[14] fugitive from Jerusalem by the name of Jonathan led a large number of poor Jewish people into the wilderness of Cyrene, "promising them a display of signs and apparitions" (Josephus, *War* 7:11, 1), which were to serve as omens of their coming messianic liberation. Three thousand of his followers were killed by Roman swords. Jonathan himself, upon command of Caesar Vespasian, was tortured and burned alive. During the years 115–117 a "messianic king" headed the rebel movement in Cyrene. However, after a short-lived success he too experienced the same fate as his predecessors.

Things did not go better for the Jewish "prophet from Egypt" who, according to Acts 21:38, was able to attract some 4000 believers—Josephus gives the figure as 30,000 (*War* 2: 261-263)—who accompanied him through the wilderness of Judea to the Mount of Olives, from where he hoped to enter Jerusalem by force. Felix, the governor, attacked the column with his troops and slaughtered most of the Jews. The "Egyptian," however, was able to escape with a small band; this gave rise to the legend alluded to in Acts 21:38, that he had ascended to heaven, whence he would shortly return.

The last rebellion against the Roman empire was mounted in the year 132 by Simon bar Kochba, who was publicly proclaimed Messiah by Rabbi Akiba, the leading scholar of his time.

The blow that finally silenced the cry for pseudo-messianic liberation for several generations occurred some three years later, when the "Son of the Star," as bar Kochba was called, along with several thousand of his comrades in arms, fell at the hands of the Roman legions and was unmasked as the "Son of lies" *(bar Kozeba)* by the sorely afflicted rabbis.

At the turn of the century, messianic enthusiasts and radicals haunted by the imminent threat of the last day had not only introduced an excess of misfortune and tragedy into Judaism, but brought all Israel to the brink of destruction.

The prophecy of Matt. 24:9ff., "Many false prophets will arise and lead many astray. . . . They will deliver you up to tribulation, and put you to death," has its roots in this experience. Most of these "messiahs" used the messianic assertion, "I am the Messiah," far more arrogantly and autocratically than Jesus, who never applied these portentious words to himself.

Now many will object that, though this is true, Peter's confession still speaks directly of Jesus as the Messiah. This passage, which comes to us in three versions (Mark 8:27-30; Matt. 16:13-23; Luke 9:18-22), reveals much more than is generally realized.

"Who do men say that I am?" is the opening question Jesus asks his disciples. It was a Jewish question, directed by a Jew to his fellow Jewish believers, which in good Jewish fashion elicited a series of different responses. He is John the Baptist, was one opinion; he is Elijah, was another; according to a third view he could be Jeremiah, while others were content to view him as "one of the prophets."

In other words, at the conclusion of his Galilean ministry, after he had, as we are repeatedly told, preached in "all the synagogues" in his homeland for several years,[15] none of the people who knew him considered Jesus to be the Messiah or the Son of God or the Savior of Israel, in whatever form. And among the Twelve only one is prepared to confess, "You are the Messiah," as Mark reports (Mark 8:27f.), to which Matthew adds, "the Son of the living God" (Matt. 16:16). Luke devises a compromise formula, "the Messiah of God," by combining the two (Luke 9:20). In John's Gospel, Peter merely calls Jesus "the Holy One of God" (John 6:69), which has no messianic ring whatsoever to it.

None of the other 11 disciples add their assent to Peter's confession; more strikingly we hear of no direct approval of Jesus. To the contrary, almost immediately Jesus bluntly rebukes Peter, "Get behind me Satan!" Already Augustine considered this worthy of thought: "The very Peter, called blessed one moment, is called Satan the next."[16]

Not everyone will agree with Bultmann's solution: "The scene of Peter's confession (Mark 8:27-30) . . . is an Easter story projected backward into Jesus' lifetime."[17]

Eduard Schweizer expresses another opinion: "Since Jesus could not possibly have announced the details of his passion and resurrection (Mark 8:31) in the form recorded—if he had, the complete confusion of the disciples on Good Friday would be incomprehensible—many scholars have suggested that Jesus' sharp rebuke of Peter (8:32-33) historically followed directly after the latter's statement, 'You are the Messiah.' This would mean that Jesus completely rejected the title."[18]

Oscar Cullmann, who emphasizes that on the way to Caesarea Philippi Jesus neither agrees nor disagrees with Peter when he says to him, "You are the Messiah," proposes that Matt. 16:13-25 "should not carry the title, 'Peter's Confession,' but rather 'Rejection of the Satanic Messiah Conception.' " In his confession, Peter "thought of the political Messiah, who was not meant to suffer."[19]

From a Jewish perspective, it is incomprehensible that the

same Peter who confessed Jesus as Messiah could continue to address him simply as "Rabbi" or "Master" (Mark 9:5 and other passages), deny him three times (Mark 26:69-75), and, after Good Friday, seek his own deliverance by taking flight.

On the other hand, the continuing ignorance of the people regarding a messiahship known only to Peter makes sense, since Jesus expressly prohibits his disciples from telling anyone about it. In my opinion there is no convincing argument to deny the historicity of the statement, "And he charged them to tell no one about him" (Mark 8:30; the parallel passages are similarly formulated in Matt. 16:20 and Luke 9:21).

Moreover, Jesus' command to keep silent included the evil spirits who, so it appears, had a particular sense for his heavenly origin: "He . . . cast out many demons; and he would not permit the demons to speak, because they knew him" (Mark 1:34), namely, as "the Holy One of God" (Mark 1:24), a title which could in no way be understood as messianic.

"Whenever the unclean spirits beheld him, they fell down before him and cried out, 'You are the Son of God,' " which in Hebrew and in Aramaic does not necessarily have anything to do with messianism. "And he strictly ordered them not to make him known" (Mark 3:11f.). "And demons also came out of many, crying, 'You are the Son of God!' But he rebuked them, and would not allow them to speak, because they knew that he was the Christ" (Luke 4:41).

Jesus' repeated command to those he had healed to keep the miracle a secret is equally striking: "And a leper came to him beseeching him, and kneeling said to him, 'If you will, you can make me clean.' Moved with pity, he stretched out his hand and touched him, and said to him, 'I will; be clean.' And immediately the leprosy left him, and he was made clean" (Mark 1:40-41).

The sudden transition from compassion to something that almost approaches an outburst of anger is unusual: "And he [Jesus] sternly charged him, and sent him away at once, and said to him, 'See that you say nothing to anyone' " (Mark 1:40ff.).

After the raising of Jairus' daughter it is reported that "he strictly charged them that no one should know this" (Mark 5:43). The blind man of Bethsaida whose sight he had restored he charges, "Do not even enter the village" (Mark 8:26). The two blind men whose "eyes were opened" he "sternly charged," saying, "see that no one knows it" (Matt. 9:30). And later it is said quite generally, "And many followed him, and he healed them all, and ordered them not to make him known" (Matt. 12:15).

In remarkable contrast to this seal of strictest secrecy is the healing of the Gerasene demoniac, from whom he had driven a "legion" of demons: "And as he was getting into the boat, the man who had been possessed with demons begged him that he might be with him. But he [Jesus] refused, and said to him, 'Go home to your friends, and tell them how much the Lord has done for you, and how much he has had mercy on you' " (Mark 5:18f.). With this it is obvious that the miraculous healing is not attributed to Jesus but to God—an exception which Jesus' words to the woman with an issue of blood corroborate: "Daughter, your faith has made you well" (Mark 5:34).

How little such healings had to do with messiahship in popular belief is demonstrated by the reaction of the crowds, as soon as they heard of it:

- "And all men marveled" (Mark 5:20).
- "And immediately they were overcome with amazement" (Mark 5:42).

- "And the crowds marveled" (Matt. 9:33).
- "And they were astonished beyond measure, saying, 'He has done all things well' " (Mark 7:37).

Repeatedly the people thank, not Jesus, but the true source of his healing deeds. So, for example, it is reported after the healing of the lame man that "When the crowds saw it, they were afraid, and they glorified God, who had given such authority to men" (Matt. 9:8). The text does not mention the Son of man, but refers simply to "men," human beings as such. Following the mass healing of "the lame, the maimed, the blind, the dumb, and many others," we hear, "And they glorified the God of Israel" (Matt. 15:30f.).

The transfiguration is even more significant. It is described as a visionary experience of the three principal disciples in which Jesus himself does not play an active role. Here, precisely where "divine sonship" is the issue, as verified by a voice from heaven which combines three Old Testament quotations,[20] Jesus "charged them to tell no one what they had seen, until the Son of man should have risen from the dead. So they kept the matter to themselves, questioning what the rising from the dead meant" (Mark 9:9f.).

In the last sentence another factor comes to the fore which is often stressed in the Gospels: the disciples' lack of understanding concerning Jesus' veiled allusion to his passion. This was for them—as it was for all Israel—incompatible with messianism.[21] Luke's comment after Jesus' second prediction of his passion is characteristic: "But they [the disciples] did not understand this saying, and it was concealed from them, that they should not perceive it; and they were afraid to ask him about this saying" (Luke 9:45).

Moreover, it is reported that, "he [Jesus] told them many things in parables" (Matt. 13:3); that "all this Jesus said to the crowds in parables," and that "he said nothing to them without a parable" (Matt. 13:34). "Why do you speak to them in parables?" (Matt. 13:10), his disciples asked him one day. He replied, "To you it has been given to know the secrets of the kingdom of heaven, but to them [the crowds] it has not been given. . . . This is why I speak to them in parables, because seeing they do not see, and hearing they do not hear, nor do they understand" (Matt. 13:10ff.). Mark formulates the reply of Jesus even more extremely: "For those outside [the crowds] everything is in parables; *so that* they may indeed see but not perceive, and may indeed hear but not understand; lest they should turn again and be forgiven" (Mark 4:11f.).

Even if the so-called "hardening theory" (that Jesus all but sadistically intended to exclude the broad masses of people from the kingdom of God by leading them astray) is attributed to the redaction of the Evangelists it still remains certain that Jesus preferred preaching in parables which deliberately refrain from reference to details concerning the "when" and "how" of the coming of the kingdom of heaven, so common in popular parlance. Joachim Jeremias, among others, makes this clear, particularly in his exposition of the numerous reinterpretations, "clarifications," misuses, and misunderstandings which the metaphors of Jesus have undergone since the very beginning of the church.[22]

Just what the parables as a whole were intended to convey and where the original sense of their message can be found still remains debatable. What impression did they make on those who heard Jesus? Repeatedly we are confronted by the same course of events: Jesus speaks to the public; he is evidently not understood or misunderstood, whereupon he discloses the deeper meaning of his puzzling words within the familiar circle of his disciples.[23] And even then, he at times rebukes his own disciples, "Do you not yet perceive or understand? Are your hearts hardened? Having eyes do you not see, and having ears do you not hear?" (Mark 8:17ff.).

Indeed, even after the resurrection and following Jesus' appearance "to them during forty days, and speaking of the kingdom of God" (Acts 1:3), the disciples still seem not to have understood the "mysterious suffering" of a crucified Messiah. The last question they ask before his ascension unwaveringly reflects the old and popular idea of a liberating kingly Messiah: "Lord, will you at this time restore the kingdom to Israel?" (Acts 1:6).

If the intimate circle of the Twelve were not capable of grasping the secret of the "suffering Messiah" despite repeated instructions from Jesus himself and if their lack of understanding could outlive even Golgotha, as their despair and panic-stricken Good Friday flight so eloquently testify, then how can one possibly expect such an understanding from the broad masses of the people of Israel at the time, particularly since to them the idea of a suffering Messiah would have seemed an absurd contradiction! All the more since Jesus never revealed himself publicly as the Messiah, and strictly forbade others to describe him as such. And, as if this were not enough, his consistent practice of concealment—whether it was actually his own or that of the evangelists makes little difference—is matched by a fundamental avoidance of any form of public acclaim that might have led to the acceptance of his possible messiahship. When the news of his healings and his preaching began to spread throughout Galilee, we read: "In the morning, a great while before day, he rose and went out to a lonely place, and there he prayed. And Simon and those who were with him followed him, and they found him and said to him,

'Every one is searching for you.' And he said to them, 'Let us go on to the next towns . . . ' "(Mark 1:35ff.).

"Now when he heard that John had been arrested, he withdrew into Galilee" (Matt. 4:12).

"Now when Jesus heard this, he withdrew from them in a boat to a lonely place apart" (Matt. 14:13).

"But so much the more the report went abroad concerning him; and great multitudes gathered to hear and to be healed of their infirmities. But he withdrew to the wilderness . . ." (Luke 5:15f.).

"They went on from there and passed through Galilee. And he would not have any one know it" (Mark 9:30).

No wonder that at the time of his entrance into Jerusalem most people do not seem to recognize him and have to ask, "Who is this?" (Matt. 21:10).

The clearest indication of Jesus' avoidance of messianic or quasi-messianic acknowledgment is found in the Fourth Gospel: "When the people saw the sign which he had done, they said, 'This is indeed the prophet who is to come into the world!' Perceiving then that they were about to come and take him by force to make him king, Jesus withdrew *again* to the hills by himself" (John 6:15).

Albert Schweitzer wondered how Jesus could "abandon . . . a people so anxious to learn and so eager for salvation."[24] He continued: "Of His 'public ministry,' . . . a large section falls out, being cancelled by a period of inexplicable concealment." Already in the early days of his ministry several signs indicate that he had "at most a quite transient contact with the people." Jesus' actions "suggests a doubt whether He really felt Himself to be a 'teacher.' "[25]

One can also detect the editorial hand of later messiologists in the account of Jesus' entrance into Jerusalem. It is certain that the cry *Hosanna* as well as the bearing of palm branches (John 12:13) belong to the ritual of the feast of tabernacles,[26] and that the cry of the masses, according to Mark 11:10, is "Blessed is the kingdom of our father David," not "his father David," but "*our* father David," that is, the father of all the children of Israel. It is just as clear that the cries, "Save us, we beseech thee, O Lord" (Hosanna) are from Ps. 118:25 and, together with the following verse (Ps. 118:26), "Blessed be he who enters in the name of the Lord!" also belonged to the appointed ritual with which the citizens of Jerusalem were accustomed to greeting the pilgrims who came from abroad.[27]

So Albert Schweitzer can conclude: Even if, at the entrance into Jerusalem, the participants according to Matt. 21:9 present their Hosannas to the son of David, in doing so they have no thought of offering him a messianic ovation. "In Matthew . . . the Galilean Passover pilgrims, after the 'Messianic entry,' answer the question of the people of Jerusalem as to who it was whom they were acclaiming, with the words 'this is the Prophet Jesus from Nazareth of Galilee' (Matt. 21:11)." Concerning Mark's description Albert Schweitzer wrote: "According to Havet, Brandt, Wellhausen, Dalman, and Wrede the ovation at the entry had no Messianic character whatever. . . . Was Mark conscious, one wonders, that it was not a Messianic entry that he was reporting? We do not know."[28]

Now let us turn to the trial of Jesus which has at its center the question of the Messiah. Of the many problems that are occasioned by the controversial and at times contradictory descriptions of the evangelists, Albert Schweitzer lists several of the most significant: "How does the High Priest know that Jesus claimed to be the Messiah? And why does he put the accusation as a direct question without calling witnesses in support of it? Why was the attempt first made to bring up a saying about the Temple which could be interpreted as blasphemy in order to condemn Him on this ground (Mark 14:57-59)? Before that again, as is evident from Mark's account, they had brought up a whole crowd of witnesses in the hope of securing evidence sufficient to justify His condemnation; and the attempt had not succeeded. It was only after all these attempts had failed that the High Priest brought his accusation concerning the Messianic claim, and he did so without citing the three necessary witnesses. Why so? Because he had not got them. The condemnation of Jesus depended on His own admission."[29]

So the high priest turns to Jesus with the question, "Are you the Messiah?" Mark adds the words, "the Son of the Blessed" (14:61), a description which is unthinkable in Hebrew or Aramaic, and must therefore be a later addition.[30] In Matthew (26:63), by contrast, the question reads, "I adjure you by the living God tell us if you are the Christ, the Son of God." The sworn declaration Jesus is asked to make on his own behalf is unknown in rabbinic tradition, which in such instances is closer to Jesus' own teaching: "Do not swear at all, either by heaven, for it is the throne of God, or by the earth, for it is his footstool . . ." (Matt. 5:34f.).

And if swearing under oath contradicts Jewish practice of the time, so does the question concerning God's Son which is posed separately in Luke (22:70); it simply cannot be imagined as coming from the mouth of a Jewish high priest. It is commonly known that the designation *Son of God* in Hebrew has nothing to do with the same Greek phrase used much later as a confession of faith; nor was its self-avowal punishable under Jewish law. Only in Mark (14:62) does Jesus give an affirmative answer, "I am," to the Messiah question. Matthew (26:64) deliberately formulates the reply ambiguously, "You have said so," which we recognize from rabbinic literature as an evasion.[31] Luke contents himself with an even more evasive answer, "You say that I am" (22:70). Completely aside from the fact that it would have been historically impossible to obtain an exact report of the proceedings of this closed hearing, it is clear that the evangelists were "dissatisfied" with the reply of Jesus held by the first generation of Jewish Christians and in various ways attempted to "improve" it.

Nevertheless the three Synoptics fully agree on one of Jesus' statements, "You will see the Son of man sitting at the right hand of Power, and coming with the clouds of heaven" (Mark 14:62). However one interprets these hotly disputed words, it remains certain that Jesus here speaks of the future, and in the third person; in other words, he implies that the prophecies of Ps. 110:1 and Dan. 7:13 would, according to a then popular interpretation, soon be fulfilled—without ever intimating that he himself would be involved.

It is for this reason that the two statements of Mark seem to be self-contradictory to Jewish ears, "I am; and you will see the Son of man . . ." (Mark 14:62).

If the Son of man (as Messiah) is *still* to come, then Jesus cannot be the Messiah. And if Jesus already is the Messiah, there is no necessity of a future savior who is still to come.

But the principal question remains unanswered: If Jesus was in fact the Messiah of Israel sent by God, why should it be the elite of the priests—of all people—who reject this bringer of salvation, to say nothing of turning him over to the Gentile rulers?

To paraphrase Paul's words, if they had recognized Jesus as the Messiah, they would not have delivered "the Lord of glory" to the Romans, but would instead have anointed and crowned him themselves (1 Cor. 2:8). In other words, whatever Jesus of Nazareth became for the little band of Jews who witnessed his resurrection, and later for the Gentile church, he was not perceived as the Messiah of Israel by the Jewish people.

Another state of affairs cannot be dismissed out of hand: Even though Jesus refrained from predicting the exact moment when the messianic age would begin, his expectation of its coming was still so intensive and certain, that he could portray time as having all but run out for this world. Accordingly he said that some of his disciples would "not taste death before they see the Son of man coming in his kingdom" (Matt. 16:28), that they would not have completed their mission in Israel "before the Son of man comes" (Matt. 10:23), and that the judgment of God would be required "of this generation" (Luke 11:51). "Truly, I say to you," he declares prophetically to his disciples, "this generation will not pass away before all these things take place" (Mark 13:30).

It would require a weighty anthology to gather all of the interpretations of skilled exegetes, who have tried, by all means at their disposal, to explain away the fact that these prophecies have not come true. The question whether these sayings come from the mouth of Jesus or from the early church, or can perhaps be attributed to the evangelists, has in the meanwhile been answered almost unanimously: these predictions must belong to the oldest tradition, since no one who believed in Jesus would have fabricated sayings that could only serve to embarrass the church.[32] After 1900 years, the nonfulfillment of Jesus' proclamation of the end-time has finally and conclusively been declared; thus the beginning of the ongoing delay of the parousia was set back into the life of Jesus itself.

Rudolf Bultmann is quite frank in expressing the consequences: "Of course, Jesus was mistaken in thinking that the world was destined soon to come to an end."[33]

Werner Georg Kümmel, who bases his conclusions on the findings of other authors, is no less direct: "It is perfectly clear that this prediction of Jesus was not realized and it is therefore impossible to assert that Jesus was not mistaken about this."[34]

This appears to be generally accepted in theological circles. The Catholic dogmatician Karl Rahner is also of the opinion that "one can speak of an error concerning Jesus' expectation of the last day, for in this error he merely shared our lot, since it is better for historical beings, and so also for Jesus, to err than it is always to know everything."[35]

Hans Küng expresses himself similarly: "Is not Jesus ultimately an apocalyptic fanatic? Was he not under an illusion? In a word, was he not mistaken? Strictly speaking, we need not have any dogmatic inhibitions about admitting this in certain circumstances. To err is human. And if Jesus of Nazareth was truly man he could also err."[36]

Finally, to admit this error diminishes neither Jesus' magnanimity nor his spiritual attraction. Even Rabbi Akiba, one of the brightest lights of Israel, made a messianic mistake in declaring Bar Kochba the Messiah of Israel (p.Taan. 68d), only a century after Golgotha. But isn't it at least conceivable that anyone—be it Jesus or Akiba—who makes a mistake in such a vital matter as redemption could err also in other matters such as assertions about themselves, reproaches of others, or biblical interpretations?

We can *summarize* as follows:

There are five good reasons why the masses of Jewish people in Israel at the turn of the age, even with the best of intentions, could not have recognized Jesus as their Messiah:

1. He did not publicly appear as such.
2. He expressly forbade his disciples and all those who knew him to reveal the secret of his passion.

3. He repeatedly avoided all acclamation by the people, often withdrawing "to a place apart," in order to seek solitude; and he performed most of his healings under the seal of strict secrecy.
4. His parables concerning salvation conceal rather than reveal the details of the coming kingdom of heaven; and the original meaning of most of his parables about the last days is disputed to this day.
5. If it is true, as Paul says, "How are they to believe in him of whom they have never heard?" (Rom. 10:14), then it is equally true that the greater majority of the Jewish people of the time neither believed in Jesus nor could have become "Christians" because they had never heard anything at all about Jesus.

These facts are all known by theologians and are slowly beginning to be circulated even among nontheologians. So Eduard Schweizer writes: "Argument has raged for decades over whether Jesus himself thought he was the Messiah. . . . Nevertheless, there is not a single genuine saying of Jesus in which he refers to himself as the Messiah."[37]

Ernst Käsemann is of a similar opinion: "Does this mean that he [Jesus] understood himself to be the Messiah? . . . I personally am convinced that there can be no possible grounds for answering this question in the affirmative. I consider all passages in which any kind of Messianic prediction occurs to be kerygma shaped by the community."[38]

Franz Mussner, the Catholic New Testament scholar from Regensburg, writes, "Christology is nothing other than a way of speaking about Jesus. . . . Reflecting on the wealth of one's experiences with Jesus leads to the objectivizing of a single aspect of this fullness which is then expressed verbally in a particular title or phrase. For example, the disciples expressed Jesus' announcement of God's rule in the title *Messiah,* because the "kingdom of God" and "Messiah" belong together."[39]

If Jesus was not the Messiah of Israel, the portrayal of Judaism by the church, its teachers, exegetes, and catechists requires a fundamental revision. For 1900 years "the Jews" have been regarded as "unbelievers" by the church—because they remained true to their faith, which was also the faith of Jesus.

Why should "the kingdom of God . . . be taken away from the Jews and given to a nation producing the fruits of it" (Matt. 21:43), when we have neither rejected the kingdom of God nor its heralds? Do not then the notorious "woes" (Matt. 23:32-39), at least insofar as they are directed against Judaism as a whole, have to be unmasked as spiteful interpolations of the post-Jesus period, and as a betrayal of Jesus' command of universal love?

Is not now the entire theological basis for that Johannine dualism removed, which accuses the Jews of being children of "the devil" (John 8:44) and denounces them as the epitome of unbelief and darkness? And what about the absolutism of the Christological claim, expressed most sharply in John 14:6 and Acts 4:12, which since early catholicism has led to a form of anti-Judaic salvation chauvinism that assigns judgment to Israel and grace to the church?

If Jesus of Nazareth was not the Messiah of Israel, we have not "stumbled over the stumbling stone" (Rom. 9:32); our hearts have not been "hardened" (Rom. 11:7); God did not give us "a spirit of stupor" (Rom. 11:8); we experienced no "failure" or "rejection" (Rom. 11:12 and 15); nor have we become "enemies of God" regarding the gospel (Rom. 11:28). We do not read our Bible through "a veil" (2 Cor. 3:15) but "with unveiled face" (2 Cor. 3:18) and clear eyes, for God has in no way "blinded" our minds (2 Cor. 4:4), nor have we been "consigned . . . to disobedience (Rom. 11:25f.).

We are and remain Israelites, to whom "belong the sonship, the glory, the covenants, the giving of the law, the worship, and the promises" (Rom. 9:4)—promises that have not yet been fulfilled, and for whose realization we continue undauntedly to hope.

Those who read the Gospels with Jewish eyes cannot avoid the impression that Jesus was not only the victim of a judicial murder, but that after his death he also fell prey to the biblical fidelity of his evangelists. It is due primarily to their editorial adeptness that more than 60 passages and prophetic words in the Hebrew Bible were twisted to prove Jesus' messiahship at every turn.

The virgin birth is derived from an erroneous Greek translation *(parthenos)* of Isa. 7:14, where the original Hebrew clearly says, "Behold, a young woman *(almah)* shall conceive and bear a son, and shall call his name Immanuel."

The birthplace, Bethlehem, comes from the prophecy of Micah (5:2) which Matthew again quotes from the inaccurate Greek translation, "And you, O Bethlehem, in the land of Judah, are by no means least among the rulers of Judah; for from you shall come a ruler who will govern my people Israel" (Matt. 2:6).

Regarding the flight of Jesus and his parents to Egypt, Matthew (2:15) resorts to a quotation from Hosea (11:1), "Out of Egypt have I called my son." But this passage actually speaks of the whole people of Israel as God's "first-born son" (Exod. 4:22) and of their exodus from Egypt.

So too, thousands of children are said to have been murdered in Bethlehem in order that Matthew (2:16ff.) can follow Jeremiah (31:15) and let their mothers lament like "Rachel weeping for her children." Jesus is reported to have entered Jerusalem riding on two beasts, because the same evangelist took the biblical parallels of Zech. 9:9 about "riding on an ass, on a colt the foal of an ass" all too literally. And Pilate, the Gentile Roman governor was obliged to wash his hands in good Old Testament fashion because King David once said (Ps. 26:6), "I wash my hands in innocence."

The "gorgeous" white robe in which Jesus was arrayed by Herod (Luke 23:11) was meant to show that he was the true high priest; just as the "scarlet robe" in which he was clothed by the soldiers who mocked him was meant to demonstrate his kingship. It is also reported that Jesus changed garments upon the celebration of his sacrificial death, just as the high priest did on the day of atonement. For ears attuned to the Bible, this signified that from then on Jesus' atoning death was to replace the day of atonement.

Jesus had to be betrayed by one of those at table with him because the psalmist said, "Even my bosom friend in whom I trusted, who ate of my bread, has lifted his heel against me" (Ps. 41:9). In the same way, the kiss of Judas is prefigured by King David, whose general Joab treacherously killed his rival Amasa with the sword while Amasa was kissing him (2 Sam. 20:9). For his "betrayal" Judas must receive "thirty pieces of silver" (Matt. 27:3)—a type of currency which was no longer used at Jesus' time—only because the book of Exodus (21:32) speaks of "thirty shekels of silver" as the cheapest price for which a man could be bought—the value of a slave, which

Zechariah later mockingly relates to his own condition (Zech. 11:12f.).

Evidently the book of Isaiah was the force behind Jesus' being scourged, spat upon, and mocked, since the suffering servant of God (Isa. 50:6; 53:5ff.) was subjected to the same humiliations. Jesus had to endure thirst (Ps. 22:16; John 19:28) and drink gall (Matt. 27:34) and vinegar (John 19:29) because the psalmist had received such repulsive food from his persecutors (Ps. 69:22). He had to die between "two robbers" (Matt. 27:38), in order that the Scripture might be fulfilled, "He was reckoned with the transgressors" (Mark 15:28; Isa. 53:9ff.). It was also necessary for him to be buried with the rich (Isa. 53:9; Matt. 27:57-60). And since Ps. 22:19 says, "They parted my garments among them, and for my clothing they cast lots," it was important that the Roman soldiers divide his garments among themselves, and cast lots for his seamless tunic.

The same legionnaires were not allowed to break his legs (John 19:33), the customary way of putting an end to the agony of the crucified, since the breaking of bones was forbidden in connection with the eating of the Passover lamb (Exod. 12:46). However, they had to thrust a spear into his side (John 19:34), since the prophet Zechariah in a disputed passage says, "When they look on him whom they have pierced, they shall mourn for him" (Zech. 12:10).

And so it goes on from the inscription Pilate had placed over the cross to the scoffing of bystanders along the way to Golgotha; from the "hyssop" held to his mouth by a Roman centurion to his last word from the cross, which is a direct quotation from Ps. 22:1.

There is virtually no point or particular in the gospel accounts which is not influenced by this adherence to biblical literalism, so much so that the seemingly desperate search for the "scriptural fulfillment" of every detail often sounds more ritualistic than real, even when actual events are at least partly involved. Concerning this mania for parallelism, the Protestant New Testament scholar Markus Barth says: "We acknowledge that ever since the first century after Christ's birth Christians have sought out, collected, and repeated passages from the Hebrew Bible in an attempt to prove the messiahship of Jesus to the Jews. . . . But this has done neither them nor the Jews any good."[40] Why? Because the Jews are "hardened"; have their eyes "veiled"; are struck with "blindness"—so runs the classical answer of the church fathers, which is still echoed today.

But the response of Judaism is more faithful to the Bible, because all the approximately 60 references to "scriptural fulfillment" in the life and death of Jesus, often recognizable as editorial glosses, pale in their significance for salvation when one compares them with the essential prophecies of the prophets of Israel that are to be fulfilled upon the arrival of the Messiah. And all of these, only some of which shall be listed, await their realization to this very day:

1. *The conversion of all Gentiles*
   Thus says the Lord of hosts: In those days ten men from the nations of every tongue shall take hold of the robe of a Jew, saying, "Let us go with you, for we have heard that God is with you" (Zech. 8:23).

2. *The pilgrimage of the nations to Jerusalem*
   Then every one that survives of all the nations that have come against Jerusalem shall go up year after year to worship the King, the Lord of hosts, and to keep the feast of booths (Zech. 14:16).

3. *The end of all idolatry*
And on that day, says the Lord of hosts, I will cut off the names of the idols from the land, so that they shall be remembered no more; and also I will remove from the land the prophets and the unclean spirit (Zech. 13:2).

4. *The revelation of God's worldwide kingdom*
And the Lord will become king over all the earth; on that day the Lord will be one and his name one (Zech. 14:9).

5. *The end of proselytism*
And no longer shall each man teach his neighbor and each his brother, saying, "Know the Lord," for they shall all know me, from the least of them to the greatest, says the Lord; for I will forgive their iniquity, and I will remember their sin no more (Jer. 31:34).

6. *Concord among all believers*
Yea, at that time I will change the speech of the peoples to a pure speech, that all of them may call on the name of the Lord and serve him with one accord (Zeph. 3:9).

7. *The establishment of Jerusalem as the center of a global ecumene*
It shall come to pass in the latter days that the mountain of the house of the Lord shall be established as the highest of the mountains, and shall be raised above the hills; and all the nations shall flow to it, and many peoples shall come, and say: "Come, let us go up to the mountain of the Lord, to the house of the God of Jacob; that he may teach us his ways and that we may walk in his paths." For out of Zion shall go forth the law, and the word of the Lord from Jerusalem (Isa. 2:2-3).

8. *The threefold covenant between Israel and its neighbors*
In that day Israel will be the third with Egypt and Assyria, a blessing in the midst of the earth, whom the Lord of hosts has blessed, saying, "Blessed be Egypt my people,

and Assyria the work of my hands, and Israel my heritage" (Isa. 19:24).

9. *The end of torment for all animals*
And I will make for you a covenant on that day with the beasts of the field, the birds of the air, and the creeping things of the ground; and I will abolish the bow, the sword, and war from the land; and I will make you lie down in safety (Hos. 2:18).

10. *The reunification of Israel under God*
Thus says the Lord God: Behold, I will take the people of Israel from the nations among which they have gone, and will gather them from all sides, and bring them to their own land; and I will make them one nation in the land, upon the mountains of Israel. . . . They shall not defile themselves any more with idols and their detestable things, or with any of their transgressions; but I will save them from all the backsliding in which they have sinned, and will cleanse them; and they shall be my people, and I will be their God (Ezek. 37:21ff.).

11. *The messianic kingdom of peace*
The wolf shall dwell with the lamb, and the leopard shall lie down with the kid, and the calf and the lion and the fatling together, and a little child shall lead them. The cow and the bear shall feed; their young shall lie down together; and the lion shall eat straw like the ox. The suckling child shall play over the hole of the asp, and the weaned child shall put his hand on the adder's den. They shall not hurt or destroy in all my holy mountain; for the earth shall be full of the knowledge of the Lord as the waters cover the sea (Isa. 11:6-9).

None of the schools of Judaism maintained that the Messiah had to come to this world in Bethlehem (Matt. 2:lff.), flee to

Egypt (Matt. 2:13ff.), be a Nazarene (Matt. 2:23), enter Jerusalem on the foal of an ass (Matt. 21:lff.), be betrayed by a Judas for 30 pieces of silver (Matt. 26:14f.; 27:9), be denied by a Peter (Matt. 26:69ff.), or be condemned by a Pilate (Matt. 27:24ff.) in order to suffer an inevitable and torturous atoning death (John 19:28ff.). No Torah-faithful Jew can believe in the beginning of the messianic age until the 11 prophecies mentioned above are visibly fulfilled on the public stage of world history.

"For truly, I say to you, till heaven and earth pass away, not an iota, not a dot, will pass from the law until all is accomplished" (Matt. 5:18).

This "all," with which Jesus undergirds the eternal validity of the Torah, also encompasses all of these as yet unfulfilled prophecies. The realization of this abundance of outstanding promises is indispensable to the vision of the end-time.

Indispensable—for if our contemporary world, with its genocide, racial hatred, and threat of atomic war, is already living in a messianic age, which considers the dawn of salvation to be behind it, then our faith is in vain, and our hope for deliverance is empty delusion.

If this divided, incomplete, and incredulous world has already experienced redemption then this life is indeed a dreadful vale of tears, and it would be better not to have been born.

Still Jesus, if I understand him rightly, was neither an illusionist regarding fulfillment nor a triumphalist regarding salvation, but rather, like many Jews, an incorrigible optimist and hero of faith, whose entire striving was directed toward the future. Like all his fellow believers it was precisely the miserable, unredeemed condition of this world, that kindled his vibrant hope—a hope in the day of the Lord which was still to come. However intensive his expectation of imminent fulfillment may have been, the Messiah remained a matter of the future throughout his life. If Jesus neither was the Messiah of Israel nor presented himself as such, only the arrival of the future Messiah remains a moot question—a parousia that has been awaited in vain for almost 2000 years.

Is it still really seriously expected at all?

Isn't it true that the church has all too easily and comfortably come to terms with this world as it is, because it seldom dreams of the world the way it ought to be? Hasn't it forgotten the hope for which the Nazarene once so vividly set an example, with his tireless proclamation of the kingdom of heaven, in which the last would be first (Mark 10:31), the least greatest (Matt. 18:4), the hungry satisfied (Luke 6:21), the heavy laden refreshed (Matt. 11:28); where the sick would be healed (Matt. 11:5), the imprisoned freed (Luke 4:18), the humble exalted (Matt. 23:12), those who mourn comforted (Matt. 5:4), and the meek would rule (Matt. 5:5)?

This kingdom of heaven in both Jewish and Christian expectation, which Jesus said was "at hand" (Mark 1:15), has not yet arrived—perhaps because we do not repent, as he and the rabbis preach: "All the predestined dates [for redemption] have passed, and the matter [now] depends only on repentance and good deeds. . . . If Israel repent, they will be redeemed; if not, they will not be redeemed."[41] Does that not sound like the call to repentance issued by the one who preached the Sermon on the Mount, who calls for deeds of "higher righteousness" because "the kingdom of God is in the midst of you" (Luke 17:21)? In Hebrew that statement can mean, "Its arrival depends on you!"

So there is hardly any other alternative than the confidence expressed by the theologian of hope, Jürgen Moltmann: "Through his crucifixion Christ has become the Saviour of the

Gentiles. But in his parousia he will also manifest himself as Israel's Messiah."[42]

That seems to me to be the basis for the discussion of an acceptable formulation of reconciliation—*until* God provides us with certainty. None of us Jews knows the identity of the One to come. Moreover, I am not certain that Christians would recognize him again if he would return to Israel as its Messiah with the same typically Jewish and rabbinic characteristics he once exhibited when he walked upon earth for some 33 years. Whether the "Son of man" Christians longingly await will be the Messiah, and whether the Messiah will be called *Joshua* (the Hebrew form of *Jesus*), none of us knows. At any rate, Jesus in the Synoptic Gospels never promised to return then or at some time in the future. And the Greek word *parousia,* which both Matthew and Paul use to designate the coming of the "Son of man," does not mean "return" but simply "arrival." This also holds true for *Maranatha* (1 Cor. 16:22), the petition with which the New Testament closes (Rev. 22:20). It does not mean "come back," but, "Our Lord, come."

And yet, God's ways remain unsearchable and who can know his sovereign saving will in advance?

We both—Jews and Christians—live in hope "until he comes," as Paul puts it (1 Cor. 11:26); we are on a pilgrimage to the same salvation, which will eliminate all our doubts and answer all our questions; and we faithfully build upon one and the same gracious love of God, without which our existence would be meaningless.

This is the threefold biblical ecumene which irrevocably binds Jews and Christians together—whether we want it or not.

Thesis Two:
The people of Israel did not reject Jesus

"He came to his own home, and his own people received him not" (John 1:11), says the prolog to the Fourth Gospel. Since the time of the early church this key passage has been interpreted, preached, and taught as the final judgment concerning Jewish "unbelief."

It is still stated similarly in numerous footnotes of the Jerusalem Bible published in 1968,[1] and in the textbooks of more than a dozen contemporary theologians for whom Judaism since the days of Jesus is nothing more than a "dead faith," a "self-righteous delusion," a "mistaken course for which they have no one but themselves to blame"; "outwardly true to the Law, but inwardly corrupt," "blind to the grace of God"; a means of "self-glorification," a "technique for atomizing religious truth"; "the great settling of accounts with God"; an "idolatry of the Law"; in short, "culpable unbelief" that "boasts in the letter of the ancient Law."[2]

Augustine considered the Jews to be an "unbelieving, stubborn, and blind people."[3] For Pope Gregory I the religion of Israel is *perfidia* or *superstitio*—unbelief or superstition— or even *perditio,* a heinous practice which "will defile the Christian faith."[4]

The leitmotif that the Jews are "faithless and hardened" because they blindly or maliciously refuse "to acknowledge their own offspring as the Messiah," occurs repeatedly in papal bulls, council pronouncements, and ecclesiastical documents until 1199 when Pope Innocent III in his *Constitutio, Licet perfidia Judaeorum* elevated Jewish "unbelief" to an article of faith: "Though for many reasons the *Perfidia* of the Jews must be condemned, nevertheless they ought not be (too) severely suppressed, for it is through them that our faith is verified *(per eos fides nostra veraciter comprobatur)"* (PL 214, 864 C-865 A).

How can the alleged unbelief of one religious community be used to support the faith of another? There is no difficulty when the power resides in the hands of the latter. By pressing "the enemies of Christ"—as Israel was preferentially titled— to the limits of annihilation and destruction, the church was able to demonstrate publicly how those would fare on earth who, as Chrysostom, the famed preacher of the fourth century declared, were "hated by God because of their unbelief."[5]

At the time of the Reformation, Erasmus of Rotterdam wrote, "If it is the business of a good Christian to hate the Jews, then we are all good Christians." In his *Dialogus inter philosophum judaeum et christianum,"* Peter Abeland (d. 1144) allows his Jewish protagonist to say, "To think that Jewish steadfastness in the midst of tribulation could go unrewarded is to declare God cruel. No other nation has suffered so much on God's behalf."

"Let us also pray for the unfaithful Jews!" So reads the translation of the Good Friday prayer which was part of every

Catholic Easter liturgy from the time of Pope Gregory the Great, around the year 600, until 1948, when Pope Pius XII permitted this petition to be "improved" by changing the word "unfaithful," which is the equivalent of a moral judgment, to "unbelieving" (*infideles in credendo*).[6]

It took another 18 years, innumerable petitions, protests, and episcopal memoranda for the Easter liturgy to be revised again. Only since Good Friday of 1976 can God be petitioned to "preserve the faithfulness of the Jews to his covenant." Nevertheless, the Latin text of the new *Missale Romanum* still contains a delicate reference to the fact that the Jewish faith leaves much to be desired: "Let us also pray for the Jews, to whom God first spoke, that they may increasingly love his name and faithfully proceed along the way God has shown them in his covenant."[7]

Why this wave of hatred, this scarlet thread that reaches from Golgotha to Auschwitz? Why this condemnation of God's biblical people, whose "perfidy" consists in remaining true to their faith through three millenia—the faith of Abraham, Moses, David, and not least, Jesus of Nazareth, who, though not the Messiah of Israel, like us, longingly hoped for the Messiah's coming?

The change in the significance of the Jewish house of prayer throughout the New Testament readily sheds light on how Jesus' belief was gradually manipulated into Jewish "unbelief": according to Luke, "he [Jesus] went to the synagogue, as his custom was, on the sabbath day. And he stood up to read" (Luke 4:16)—a practice Jesus himself confirms, "I have always taught in synagogues and in the temple, where all Jews come together" (John 18:20), and which is verified by his use of the synagogue as a primary center for proclaiming the gospel.

Next, in order to alienate Jesus from his own house of prayer, we are told that "he went about . . . teaching in *their* synagogues" (Matt. 4:23), and that "he went throughout all Galilee, preaching in *their* synagogues" (Mark 1:39).

John then speaks of "expulsion from the synagogue" (John 9:22; 12:42; 16:2): "For the Jews had already agreed that if any one should confess him [Jesus] to be the Messiah, he was to be put out of the synagogue" (John 9:22). And so the stage was set for polemical expressions such as "synagogue of Satan" (Rev. 2:9; 3:8f.), or the designation of Jews as children of their "father the devil" (John 8:44). With the break between the church and the synagogue the condemnation of "the Jews," which inevitably led to the fruits of hatred that have been harvested ever since the Middle Ages, is already in full swing.

Did the Jews really repudiate or reject Jesus? Directly after the obscure reference to "his own," who "received him not," the prolog of John says, "But to all who received him . . . he gave power to become children of God" (John 1:12). A clearer affirmation of the Jews as the children of God is actually superfluous. The resolution passed by the Third Assembly of the World Council of Churches in New Delhi on December 5, 1961, puts it this way: "The Jews were the first to receive Jesus, and the Jews are not the only ones who fail to recognize him."

It was Jews who accepted him and Jews who frequently cared for him (Matt. 25:35-36; Luke 13:31, and other references). It was in Israel that he acquired disciples whose faith in him persevered beyond his death, and led them to the conviction that the crucified one had been raised and would return soon as the Messiah. In the end the church universal is indebted to this historical complex of internal Jewish events, for its formation, for the fundamental shaping of its beliefs, and for the basis of its Holy Scripture.

Not only were the members of the mother church in Jerusalem—the initial adherents of Christendom on earth—and all of the original apostles pious Jews for whom belief in Jesus in no way conflicted with Judaism; other, far-flung circles of Jewish people also received Jesus enthusiastically. Their responses are duly recorded in the Gospels and there is no reason to doubt that this portrayal of Jesus reflects reality:

Matthew:

> And great crowds followed him from Galilee and the Decapolis and Jerusalem and Judea and from beyond the Jordan (4:25).
>
> Seeing the crowds, he went up on the mountain, and . . . opened his mouth and taught them (5:12).
>
> When Jesus finished these sayings [the Sermon on the Mount], the crowds were astonished at his teaching (7:28).
>
> When he [Jesus] came down from the mountain, great crowds followed him (8:1).
>
> Now when Jesus saw great crowds around him, he gave orders to go over to the other side (8:18).
>
> And a scribe came up and said to him, "Teacher, I will follow you wherever you go" (8:19).
>
> When the crowds saw it [the healing of the paralytic], they were afraid [that is, showed respect or stood in awe], and they glorified God, who had given such authority to men (9:8).
>
> As Jesus passed on from there, he saw a man called Matthew sitting at the tax office; and he said to him, "Follow me." And he rose and followed him (9:9).
>
> And [after the healing of the dumb man] the crowds marveled, saying, "Never was anything like this seen in Israel" (9:33).

Matthew:

When he [Jesus] saw the crowds, he had compassion for them, because they were harassed and helpless, like sheep without a shepherd (9:36).

As they [the disciples of John] went away, Jesus began to speak to the crowds concerning John (11:7).

And many followed him, and he healed them all (12:15).

And all the people were amazed, and said, "Can this be the Son of David?" (12:23).

While he [Jesus] was still speaking to the people, behold, his mother and his brothers stood outside, asking to speak to him (12:46).

And great crowds gathered about him, so that he got into a boat and sat there; and the *whole crowd* stood on the beach (13:2).

Though he [Pilate] wanted to put him [Jesus] to death, he feared *the people,* because they held him to be a prophet (14:5).

When the crowds heard it [the murder of John the Baptist], they followed him [Jesus] on foot from the towns (14:13).

As he went ashore he saw a great throng; and he had compassion on them (14:14).

And those who ate were about five thousand men, besides women and children [who are to be added to the total] (14:21).

And when the men of that place recognized him, they . . . besought him that they might only touch the fringe of his garment [the "tassels" according to Deut. 22:12] (14:36).

And he called *the people* to him and said to them . . . (15:10).

And Jesus went on from there and passed along the Sea of Galilee. And he went up into the hills, and sat down there. And great crowds came to him (15:29-30).

Matthew:

> Then Jesus . . . said, "I have compassion on the crowd, because they have been with me now three days, and have nothing to eat" (15:32).
>
> Those who ate were four thousand men, besides women and children [who are to be added to the total] (15:38).
>
> He [Jesus] went away from Galilee and entered the region of Judea beyond the Jordan; and large crowds followed him (19:1-2).
>
> As they went out of Jericho, a great crowd followed him (20:29).
>
> Most of the crowd [during Jesus' entry into Jerusalem] spread their garments on the road . . . and the crowds that went before him and that followed him shouted, "Hosanna to the Son of David!" (21:8-9).
>
> And when he entered Jerusalem, all the city was stirred, saying, "Who is this?" And the crowds said, "This is the prophet Jesus from Nazareth of Galilee" (21:10-11).
>
> When they [the chief priests and the Pharisees] tried to arrest him, they feared the multitudes, because they held him to be a prophet (21:45).
>
> When the crowd heard it, they were astonished at his teaching (22:33).
>
> Then the chief priests and the elders of the people . . . took counsel together in order to arrest Jesus by stealth and kill him. But they said, "Not during the feast, lest there be a tumult among the people" (26:3-5).
>
> There were also many women there [at the crucifixion], looking on from afar, who had followed Jesus from Galilee, ministering to him (27:55).

From Mark and Luke we shall quote only those passages that conclusively demonstrate the popularity of Jesus among the broad levels of the people of Israel:

Mark:

> And at once his fame spread everywhere throughout all the surrounding region of Galilee (1:28).
>
> And the whole city was gathered together about the door (1:33).
>
> Jesus could no longer openly enter a town [because of the crowds], but was out in the country; and people came to him from every quarter (1:45).
>
> And many were gathered together, so that there was no longer room for them, not even about the door; and he was preaching the word to them (2:2).
>
> All the crowd gathered about him, and he taught them (2:13).
>
> Many tax collectors and sinners were sitting with Jesus and his disciples; for there were many who followed him (2:15).
>
> A great multitude from Galilee followed; also from Judea and Jerusalem . . . a great multitude, hearing all that he did, came to him (3:7-8).
>
> Then he went home; and the crowd came together again, so that they could not even eat (3:19-20).
>
> Again he began to teach beside the sea. And a very large crowd gathered about him (4:1).
>
> A great crowd followed him and thronged about him (5:24).
>
> They went away in the boat to a lonely place by themselves. Now many saw them going, and knew them, and they ran there on foot from all the towns, and got there ahead of them (6:32-33).

Mark:

As he landed he saw a great throng . . . and he began to teach them many things (6:34).

He called the people to him again, and said to them, "Hear me, all of you, and understand" (7:14).

Immediately all the crowd, when they saw him [Jesus], were greatly amazed, and ran up to him and greeted him (9:15).

Crowds gathered to him again; and again, *as his custom was,* he taught them (10:1).

As he [Jesus] was leaving Jericho with his disciples and a great multitude . . . (10:46).

They [the chief priests and scribes] feared him, because *all the multitude* was astonished at his teaching (11:18).

As Jesus taught in the temple . . . the great throng heard him gladly (12:35-37).

There were also women looking on from afar [as he died] . . . who, when he was in Galilee, followed him, and ministered to him; and also many other women who came up with him to Jerusalem (15:40-41).

Luke

When they heard this [from Jesus] all the people and the tax collectors justified God (7:29).

As he said this, a woman in the crowd raised her voice and said to him, "Blessed is the womb that bore you" (11:27).

In the meantime, when so many thousands of the multitude had gathered together that they trod upon one another, he began to say . . . (12:1).

All the people rejoiced at all the glorious things that were done by him (13:17).

Now great multitudes accompanied him . . . (14:25).

Luke:

> *Now the tax collectors and sinners were all drawing near to hear him (15:1).*
>
> *All the people,* when they saw it [the healing of the blind man], gave praise to God (18:43).
>
> He [Zacchaeus] sought to see who Jesus was, but he could not, on account of the crowd (19:3).
>
> *All the people* hung upon his [Jesus'] words (19:48).
>
> He was teaching the people in the temple (20:1).
>
> And in the hearing of *all the people* he said to his disciples (20:45).
>
> Early in the morning *all the people* came to him in the temple to hear him (21:38).
>
> The chief priests and the scribes were seeking how to put him [Jesus] to death; for they feared the people . . . so he [Judas] agreed, and sought an opportunity to betray him to them in the absence of the multitude (22:2-6).
>
> There followed him [on the way of the cross] a great multitude of the people, and of women who bewailed and lamented him (23:27).
>
> All the multitudes who assembled to see the sight [of the crucifixion], when they saw what had taken place, returned home beating their breasts (23:48).

In summary we can say: In various and sundry ways, some 26 passages in Matthew, 28 in Mark, and 35 in Luke attest to the fact that large numbers of Jewish people in Galilee as well as in Judea, in Jerusalem, and in many other places were impressed by Jesus, gladly listened to him for days on end, hung on him, became his followers, accompanied him on his journeys and repeatedly welcomed him with respect and affection.

In the first three Gospels we find eight accounts in which

"the people," seven passages in which "many of the people," and five instances in which "all the people" or "the whole people," were amazed by Jesus, loved, honored, listened to and crowded around him, hung on his words, bestowed their favor upon him, and blessed or praised him. That the Gentile Gerasenes begged him "to depart from their neighborhood" (Mark 5:17), and that the Samaritans considered him *persona non grata* (Luke 9:52) merely underscores the Jewish character of his successful teaching ministry.

I know of no other figure in Jewish antiquity whose popularity and public acclaim has been attested so often and so convincingly. The same can be said of the unavoidable darker sides of life. On the whole they portray exceptions to the respect and friendship which are as a rule shown him. On one occasion people "laughed at him" (Mark 5:38); some were offended by him (Mark 6:2). He knew the proverbial disdain which every prophet experiences "among his own kin" (Mark 6:4); many of his fellow teachers rejected his often daring interpretations of Scripture, and here and there his words fell on deaf ears (Matt. 11:20ff.). All of these particulars serve only to underscore the impact of his teaching and the power of his preaching. None of Israel's heroes of faith were ever without followers and friends—or rivals and opponents.

After years of grumbling and rebellion by the children of Israel, and the attempt of Korah's followers forcefully to do away with him as the liberator of Israel, Moses complains, "How can I bear alone the weight and burden of you and your strife?" (Deut. 1:12); "I am not able to carry all this people alone, the burden is too heavy for me" (Num. 1:14).

Three times King Saul, in a jealous rage, attempted to "pin David to the wall" with a spear (1 Sam. 18:10ff. and 19:10). David had to flee for his life by night (1 Sam. 19:12). Declared an outlaw, he was pursued for years as a refugee (1 Sam. 19-27), often without food (1 Sam. 21:4ff.). It was only with great difficulty that he as the anointed king of Israel was able to escape the seditious jealousy of his own son, Absalom (2 Sam. 13–19), the rebellion of Sheba (2 Sam. 20:1–22), and the treachery and cunning of his second son, Adonijah, who, when David was "old and advanced in years," attempted to usurp his throne (1 Kings 1).

Elijah, the great zealot of God, summed up his life's mission in these words: "I have been very jealous for the Lord, the God of hosts; for the people of Israel have forsaken thy covenant, thrown down thy altars, and slain thy prophets with the sword; and I, even I only, am left; and they seek my life, to take it away" (1 Kings 19:10).

Amos, too, is exiled from the land, for as the priests say, "the land is not able to bear all his words" (Amos 7:10), Jonah is called "the ludicrous prophet," and Jeremiah is repeatedly beaten and imprisoned by the high priests (Jer. 20:2) until at last he curses the day he was born (Jer. 20:14).

So it may not only have been the fact that Jesus "taught them as one who had authority (Matt. 7:29) which led some in Israel to say he was "Elijah, and others Jeremiah or one of the prophets" (Matt. 16:14f.), but rather the hostility of the elite priests who, like so many of the prophets before him, Jesus repeatedly attacked with caustic words and symbolic acts, that eventually led to his premature death.

Markus Barth can rightly say: "Any Jew, whether a prophet, a Chasid, a wise man, a rabbi, or a Pharisee, will come into conflict with the official guardians of the Law of the day; specifically when making a radical effort to be obedient to the Law of God in word and deed, his teaching and behavior inevitably had to give offense to both the pious people and the religious establishment. To be a Jew means to bear up under and to suffer through such conflict and opposition among one's own people."[8]

Now let us turn our attention to the attitude expressed in the Fourth Gospel, an account modern biblical scholars hold to be historically unreliable. The foreword to the most recent edition of Albert Schweitzer's *The Quest of the Historical Jesus* asserts the following about this problem of New Testament research:

"The second either-or was: 'Either Synoptic or Johannine.' . . . . The Two Document Hypothesis was all the more welcome in view of the fact that the Tübingen School had drawn attention to the gnostic background of the Gospel of John, with the result that this Gospel was by and large eliminated as a historical source. In research since that time the Fourth Gospel has hardly played an important role in the question of the historical Jesus."[9]

In the same vein, the Catholic New Testament scholar Father Thomas Calmes warns: "The Fourth Gospel is the most anti-Judaic book in the New Testament. . . . Throughout it, from beginning to end, the Jews are depicted as the enemies of Jesus."[10]

That which above everything else characterizes John is a dogmatically inflexible dualism which conveniently reduces everything to black and white, splitting the entire world into abstract antitheses: light and darkness, truth and falsehood, life and death, God and the devil—but above all, Jesus and "the Jews." Erich Grässer, however, emphasizes that "to the extent to which the historical Jesus is no longer on the scene, it is also no longer the historical Jews who are his opponents."[11]

Clemens Thoma, the Catholic Judaic scholar, maintains, "The expression *the Jews* could, without falsifying the intention of the evangelist, be replaced by the expression, 'the unbelievers,' or 'the spiteful, atheistic enemies of Christ.' "[12]

So the expression *the Jews* appears only five times in Matthew and Luke, six times in Mark, but 71 times in John—almost always as the epitome of all that is evil, wicked, and unbelieving. In a word, "the Jews," as archenemies of Jesus and as "children of the devil" (John 8:44), serve as the loathsome opponents of, the dark backdrop for, and the living antithesis to the Christological "Son of God."

The evangelist himself frankly admits that this Jewish "unbelief" was not a matter of actual fact but an article of Johannine faith: "Though he had done so many signs before them, yet they did not believe in him; *it was* that the word spoken by the prophet Isaiah might be fulfilled: 'Lord, who has believed our report, and to whom has the arm of the Lord been revealed?' [Isa. 53:1]. *Therefore they could not believe.* For Isaiah again said, 'He has blinded their eyes and hardened their heart' [Isa. 6:9f.] . . ." (John 12:37-40).

To see how little this dogmatically determined "unbelief" has to do with Jesus' actual situation, we need but note the outcome reported immediately after the two Isaiah quotations upon which it is based: "Nevertheless, many even of the authorities believed in him [Jesus]" (John 12:42).

One is tempted to interject indignantly: "Either-or!" Either a doctrinal construct which for theological reasons requires Jewish unbelief—but that means dispensing with historical facts—or a plausible historical account without any abstract theological assumptions. A factual scaffolding, upon which a superstructure of dialectical Christology is imposed, cannot help but creak at the joints as soon as one examines its assertions closely.

A single example among many will suffice to show how

easily this Johannine dogma concerning Israel's unbelief can lead to a loss of credibility: "The Jews were looking for him [Jesus] at the feast, and saying, 'Where is he?' And there was much muttering about him among the people. While some said, 'He is a good man,' others said, 'No, he is leading the people astray.' Yet for fear of the Jews no one spoke openly of him" (John 7:11-13).

An Eskimo whose knowledge of Christianity came solely from the Fourth Gospel would, on the basis of such texts, have to conclude that for some unexplained reason Jesus had strayed into the evil company of treacherous, unbelieving, murderous Jews whose spitefulness would sooner or later surely cost him his life. The thought that this Jesus and "the Jews" held even the slightest thing in common would never cross his mind.

Only those who are willing to read between the lines will recognize that in the Johannine passage just quoted, "the feast" and "the people," as well as the "some" and the "others," were just as Jewish as Jesus himself. And it will begin to dawn on those who look with an open mind at what is said that there was a divided opinion in Jerusalem about Jesus and that among the elite, some of whom were also his admirers (John 12:42), there were others who accused Jesus of "leading the people astray"—a clear indication of the admiration with which the broad masses of the people regarded him.

Insights such as these moved the Vatican, in its "Guidelines and Suggestions for Implementing the Declaration of the Council, *Nostra Aetate,* paragraph 4" of January 3, 1975, to determine that "the expression, 'the Jews,' in the Gospel of John can in some contexts mean 'the leaders of the Jews' or 'the enemies of Jesus.' These expressions are better translations of the evangelist's intention and avoid the implication that the Jewish people as a whole are meant."

How great, enduring, and widespread the popularity and esteem of Jesus among his people must have been if even John, despite his own ideology, was unable to silence it completely! In fact he could not avoid mentioning it in over a dozen instances:

> Now when he was in Jerusalem at the Passover feast, many *believed* in his name" (John 2:33).
>
> They came to John [the Baptist], and said to him, "Rabbi, he who was with you [Jesus] . . . is baptizing, and *all* are going to him" (John 3:26).
>
> When he came to Galilee, the Galileans welcomed him, having seen all that he had done in Jerusalem at the feast (John 4:45).
>
> Lifting up his eyes, then, and seeing that a multitude was coming to him, Jesus said to Philip, "How are we to buy bread, so that these people may eat?" (John 6:5).
>
> When the people saw the sign which he had done, they said, "This is indeed the prophet who is to come into the world!" (John 6:14).
>
> Perceiving then that they were about to come and take him by force *to make him king,* Jesus withdrew again to the hills by himself (John 6:15).
>
> So when the people saw that Jesus was not there . . . they themselves got into the boats and went to Capernaum, seeking Jesus (John 6:24).
>
> *Many* of the people *believed* in him; they said, "When the Messiah appears, will he do more signs than this man has done?" (John 7:31).
>
> Some of the people said, "This is really the prophet." Others said, "This is the Messiah!" (John 7:40-41).

[After the officers of the chief priests and Pharisees refused to arrest Jesus] the officers answered, "No man ever spoke like this man!" The Pharisees answered them, "Are you led astray, *you also?*" (John 7:46-47).

Early in the morning he [Jesus] came again to the temple; *all the people* came to him, and he sat down and taught them (John 8:2).

As he spoke thus, *many believed* in him (John 8:30).

Jesus then said *to the Jews* who had *believed in him* (John 8:31).

And many came to him . . . and many believed in him there (John 10:41-42).

Many of the Jews therefore, who had come with Mary and had seen what he did, believed in him (John 11:45).

The chief priests and the Pharisees gathered the council, and said, "What are we to do? For this man performs many signs. If we let him go on thus, *every one will believe in him*" (John 11:47, 48).

So the chief priests planned to put Lazarus also to death, because on account of him many of the Jews were going away and believing in Jesus (John 12:10-11).

The Pharisees then said to one another, ". . . Look, the world has gone after him [Jesus]" (John 12:19).

Nevertheless many even of the authorities believed in him. . . (John 12:42).

If so many Jews accepted Jesus, followed him, attentively listened to him, believed in him, and even wanted to make him their king, despite the Johannine dogma of Jewish "unbelief," how then can the malicious hostility of "the Jews" toward Jesus, which makes it almost impossible to read this Gospel without feeling an insurmountable aversion for the entire Jewish people, be explained?

> This was why *the Jews* persecuted Jesus (John 5:16).
>
> So they took up stones to throw at him (John 8:59; 10:31).
>
> This was why *the Jews* sought all the more to kill him (John 5:18).
>
> He [Jesus] would not go about in Judea, because *the Jews* sought to kill him (John 7:1).
>
> The Jews answered him [Pilate], "We have a law, and by that law he ought to die" (John 19:7).

Certainly there must have been inveterate opponents of Jesus, especially among the rulers of the temple, who would gladly have done away with the popular but troublesome wandering preacher. Yet, may not most of the "hatred of the Jews" along with their alleged "unbelief" have arisen as a dogmatic necessity of Johannine dualism? For example, in the discourse about the hatred of the world John places the following words on Jesus' mouth: "It is to fulfil the word that is written in their law 'They hated me without a cause' " (Pss. 35:19; 69:5; John 15:25).

How do these facts square with the charge of "murdering Christ" which, after some 2000 years, still continues to serve as the root of a pseudo-theological hatred of the Jews?

"The Jews . . . killed both the Lord Jesus and the prophets" (1 Thess. 2:14-15)—so we read in one of Paul's letters in a passage considered by worthy exegetes to be an interpolation by a Gentile Christian glossator.[13] "You have now crucified the only sinless and righteous one!" says Justin to his fictional

Jewish dialog partner, Trypho, 100 years later. Origin (d. 254), assuming the position of divine judge, pronounces the final verdict: "The Jews nailed Jesus to the cross . . . therefore the blood of Jesus not only falls upon the Jews of his time, but upon every generation of Jews until the end of the world."[14]

In our own day, Hitler, following in the footsteps of innumerable church fathers, popes, and reformers could declare: "The Jews crucified Jesus; therefore they are not worthy of life."[15]

Sorry to say, similar accusations are still being made in recent theological works:

> The main responsibility rests on the Jewish side.[16]

> So they [the Jews] feel that he [Jesus] is not of one spirit with them, and do not rest until they have gotten rid of him.[17]

> It was impossible for the Jews not to be offended by Jesus. . . . Their discontent grew until it became hatred. They decided to rid themselves of this troublemaker and killed him.[18]

> By executing Christ the entire people *sealed their* rejection of God's envoy . . . , thereby subjecting themselves to the judgment under which everyone who in unbelief rejects Christ stands.[19]

> In demanding this particular mode of punishment [crucifixion], Jesus' accusers [*jüdischer* is in the original] intended to make public proclamation of three things: Slaves, rebels, and pseudo-prophets would normally be crucified. . . . The Pilate we meet in the story of the Passion is . . . a man who is making every effort to hand down a just judgment and save the life of an innocent man.[20]

> It was the [Jewish] people who crucified Jesus. . . . In this decision Israel demonstrated its unity as a community.[21]

What can be done against this flood of collective slander? "The New Testament in and of itself is not antisemitic; however, it is given an antisemitic flavor when one proclaims it without intellectually stepping back into the age of Jesus and the land of the Jews."[22] Stepping back and taking into account all historically relevant circumstances leads to the conclusion that Jesus was never tried by the Jews. John does not mention a trial before the high council; and the Synoptics, in their description of the judicial process, not only contradict each other but the Jewish legal practice of those days as well, and in eight significant points.[23]

A reconstruction of the circumstances of the time discloses that all of the nonbiblical sources accuse Pontius Pilate of brutality and corruption as well as frequently executing persons who had not been sentenced, a practice for which thousands of Jews had to pay by death on the cross. This being the case, his alleged protection of a Jew, completely unknown to him, from "the Jews," as well as the washing of his hands as a sign of innocence (Matt. 27:24), a purely Old Testament gesture (Deut. 21:6; Ps. 26:6), are historically unlikely.

Equally improbable is the so-called "self-condemnation" of "all the people" before the judgment seat of Pilate (Matt. 27:25). The previous sentence, which merely speaks of "the crowd" that had gathered, is more appropriate to the physical setting. Archaeological excavations have since established that at the most 4000 persons could have gathered in the inner court of the Antonia fortress where, according to a disputed tradition, the Roman hearing took place. The mob "stirred up" by the high priests (Mark 15:11) may have corresponded to about two percent of all the inhabitants and pilgrims staying in Jerusalem at the time—considerably less than 1/1000 of all Jews then living.

In the passion accounts "the people" are usually the followers of Jesus whom the rulers of the temple "feared." If we can believe the evangelists, their fear was justified, "because all the multitude was astonished at his teaching" (Mark 11:18). "They [the high priests and the Pharisees] feared the multitudes, because they held him to be a prophet" (Matt. 21:46). "All the people hung upon his words" (Luke 19:48). "If we [the priests] let him go on thus, every one will believe in him" (John 11:48). "They [the chief priests] said, 'Not during the feast, lest there be a tumult among the people' " (Matt. 26:5).

In other words, it was because the leaders feared Jesus that he was taken prisoner (Mark 14:43) shortly before dawn and delivered to Pilate "as soon as it was morning" (Mark 15:1).

Whoever reads the Gospels carefully and with a critical eye knows that they are not objective reports but rather statements of faith, inevitably conditioned by the spirit of the times in which they were written. They were recorded some 40 to 80 years after the crucifixion. Jerusalem had been laid waste and the Jewish people conquered, dispersed, and placed under edict throughout the Roman empire; so Jesus' Jewishness, as well as his death as a zealot at the hands of the Romans must have presented almost insurmountable dual obstacles for the newly emerging Gentile mission. As a result, it became a matter of sheer survival for the evangelists to minimize Roman responsibility for Golgotha by every possible written means, while at the same time exaggerating the guilt of "the Jews" in the death of their fellow countryman. Only in this way could they hope to mitigate the persecution of the young church by Nero and others (who came later) and convince the Roman authorities to tolerate the new religion.

Those who question this subtle editorial shift in guilt need only to compare the four different descriptions of the trial with each other in order to convince themselves how the Gospels portray the Roman procurator ever more sympathetically and "the Jews" with ever greater hostility. This shift in guilt culminates in two points: the canonization of Pilate by the Church of Ethiopia,[24] and the wholesale, collective condemnation of all Jews without due process of law, as "murderers of God."[25]

The basic facts hidden behind all of this anti-Judaic polemic are still clearly discernable to the attentive reader. The arrest of Jesus was carried out by *Roman* troops (Mark 14:43). It was *Roman* law—*lex julia majestatis*—which was applied to Jesus; only the *Roman* procurator had the authority to condemn him to death, which he did, even though he knew that Jesus was not guilty (Luke 23:4). The brutal, sadistic means of execution was *Roman* and unknown to Jewish penal law. Moreover it was *Roman* soldiers who scourged Jesus' bleeding body, spat at him, derided and humiliated him—and with him his own people—as the thorn-crowned "King of the Jews," and finally nailed his limbs to a *Roman* cross.

On the other hand, *Jews* "followed" in great numbers (Luke 23:27) as their fellow countryman climbed the hill of Golgotha. *Jewish* women attempted to ease his pain with a narcotic drink (Mark 15:23). The women who "bewailed and lamented him" were also *Jewish* (Luke 23:27), as were the multitudes who "returned home beating their breasts" in grief (Luke 23:48). Two fellow *Jews* shared his fate in death. It was *Jews* who tenderly removed Jesus' body from the cross in order to assure him a proper *Jewish* burial (Luke 23:50ff.). Finally, it was *Jews* who were the first to preach his good news; it was *Jews* to whom he appeared as the resurrected one, and it was *Jews* who founded the first churches.

Whether a Jewish hearing preceded the Roman trial, whether Jesus had to appear before the high priests, whether the

Pharisees were numbered among his opponents or whether it was only a few Sadducees who accused him before Pilate—all of these factors may be debated.[26]

Still it remains certain beyond any shadow of doubt that only some Jewish authorities—"your rulers" who "acted in ignorance," as Peter puts it (Acts 3:17)—were involved as informers in the judicial murder of Jesus, *against* the will of the people, *without* their cooperation, and *for fear* of the Jewish multitudes, who almost without exception manifested good will and affection.

Nevertheless, the tenacious, persistent, wholesale accusation of "murdering God" continues to live on to this day in hundreds of school books, in doctrinal statements, and in sermons. Johann Friedrich Konrad, a Protestant religious educator, makes the following suggestion regarding the passion history, which according to recent textbook analyses, is the embryonic source of most pedagogically transmitted anti-Judaism: "In the sovereign name of Jesus we must clearly and simply say: you have heard that it was said to those of old that the Jews killed Jesus. But I say to you, first it was the Romans who snatched Jesus from the Jews by crucifying him; and then the Christians took Jesus from the Jews by making him God! We must see to it that our children's first contact with the story of the passion is not according to the Gospel texts but rather in accord with the most plausible historical course of events. . . . The greatest and most difficult task, however, will be to write a new Christian theology or dogmatics which thinks through and describes the gospel of Jesus Christ so thoroughly that even a Jew, though he may not fully agree, can still read it without fear or bitterness, and perhaps even with joy."[27]

Regarding the role of the high priestly Sadducean aristocracy as informers in the trial of Jesus, the Protestant Old Testament scholar Walter Zimmerli cites Dostoyevski, who in his story of the Grand Inquisitor "poignantly maintains that in the end, the leadership of the Christian church would not act much differently. . . . It could well be that we are . . . so deeply alarmed by the passion account of the Gospels because we feel ourselves caught up in its inevitability."

Crucifixion, the Roman form of the death penalty, Zimmerli emphasizes, points directly to Pilate as the judicial murderer, since, according to the clear description of the Gospels, "this representative of civil justice fails in the case of Jesus Christ." The core of the gospel tradition does not conceal "that he fails to carry out the very function for which he has been appointed. He betrays the law for political opportunism. This is how the man acts, to whom political power is given. . . . This is human nature."

The Jerusalem report of the crucifixion is logically consistent in its description of the military and political executioners who crucified Jesus—as they had many other Jews. It clearly states "that the soldiers carried out their assigned task of executing Jesus with great severity. Should these executioners, who came from various places in the Roman empire also be counted among the guilty? Had they been summoned to appear in court, they would have testified that they had received their orders from above. And orders are orders. Their beating of the defenseless captive was in accord with the command they were given, and did not exceed common practice. Though there were incidents of sadism, a command was a command. Human beings as recipients of orders act that way. What is apparent in the response of these soldiers has its exact counterpart in German history as it relates to the Jews: Eichmann 'had his orders. . . .' Pilate's soldiers also speak to us: 'Humans are like that.' "[28]

Those Christians who brush aside all logical, historical, and legal arguments in order to continue their insistence upon "Jewish guilt" should read the Catechism of Trent, which was formulated by a saint of the Roman Catholic church (S. C. Borromeo) and, in the year 1570, promulgated by a canonized pope (Pius V). There we read: "Our faith teaches us: Christ the Lord was nailed on the cross during the time Pontius Pilate ruled in Judea at the command of Caesar Tiberius. . . . We must consider all those who repeatedly fall into sin as sharing the guilt; for it is because of our sins that Christ suffered death on the cross, and those who revel in sin and depravity 'crucify the Son of God on their own account and hold him up to contempt' (Heb. 6:6). Moreover, our guilt in this matter is truly greater than that of the Jews, for it is as the apostle says, 'Had they [the Jews] known this, they would not have crucified the Lord of glory' (1 Cor. 2:8); whereas we who proclaim that we have known him betray him through our deeds—we lay our hands upon him and cause him suffering."

Some four centuries ago the Catholic church already had the courage publicly to declare that in the end it is Pilate who bears the responsibility for Jesus' judicial murder; that though the whole of humanity made Jesus' sacrifice necessary through their sins, the guilt of Christians is still "greater" than that of the Jews; and that sinful Christians—which certainly includes those who slander their Jewish brothers and sisters—newly and repeatedly continue to nail Christ to the cross.

But why did the Jews not believe in him after the resurrection, which was the crowning glory of his mission? This is a valid question which requires two answers. As all of the Gospels and Paul unanimously report, Jesus' resurrection was a faith experience shared only by a few. "The revelation of the risen one took place only in the presence of chosen witnesses. Since Christ dwells {only} in the hearts of Christians through faith (Eph. 3:17), the final and visible revelation of Christ is still to come."[29]

For some, suffering and death on the cross became striking proof of the Nazarene's failure; for others, suffering and death on the cross, seen in the light of the Easter experience, were conclusive signs that God had accepted Jesus' sacrifice. The same events which brought some to despair filled those who were his with the certainty of salvation. This dual meaning is inherent to Easter faith. Was the resurrection which the disciples reported a human projection or a divinely given foretaste of eternal life? Was it merely a messianic Midrash by those who impatiently longed for the last day—or a true sign of heaven? That was the crucial question which at the time separated the followers of Jesus from their fellow Jews and later divided Jews and Christians.

A second watershed was the post-Easter metamorphosis of Jesus in the non-Jewish world. Even after the passion the admiration of the crowds and the simple faith of the Jewish people were still directed to Jesus the teacher, the preacher, the miraculous healer, the man of God mighty in words, and the prophet of Galilee, as Luke affirms:

"Jesus of Nazareth, who was a prophet mighty in deed and word before God and all the people" (Luke 24:19); "Jesus of Nazareth, a man attested to you by God with mighty works and wonders and signs which God did through him in your midst" (Acts 2:22).

How different is the predominantly Greek portrait of Christ, fashioned by Paul and John, which begins its triumphal march through the world a generation later. This savior-God, who not only had to, but wanted to die the most wretched and ignominious death in order to atone vicariously for the sins of humankind, was indeed—as Paul had to admit—"a stumbling block to Jews" (1 Cor. 1:23) but, as it soon turned out, no folly to Gentiles.

In fact he was more than a stumbling block, for this God-man of Greek alloy, who hardly had anything more than his name in common with the Jewish preacher of salvation from Galilee, could not be reconciled with Israel's basic understanding of God (Deut. 6:4ff.; Num. 23:19).

A study paper, "Christians and Jews," issued by the Protestant Church of Germany puts it this way: "In the New Testament accounts the uniqueness of Jesus Christ was . . . altered . . . . From the Jewish point of view a number of these statements seemed to jeopardize the belief in one God because they accorded Jesus all but equal status with God. By and large these were statements developed by Christian proclamation with Gentile hearers in mind. . . . To Jewish thinking these teachings increasingly appeared to be a violation of the law that no one but God was to be honored as divine."[30]

On the other hand, the earthly Nazarene—born, circumcised, and brought up as a Jew, who himself confessed the creed of Judaism (Mark 12:29), and whose life and aspiration here below was dedicated to his own people, Israel—was accorded the sympathy, admiration, and friendship of innumerable fellow believers.

So the oft-repeated testimony of all four Gospels confirms a basic and irrefutable fact: The majority of the people of Israel who were able to come into contact with Jesus gave him a warm, and often enthusiastic, reception.

Thesis Three

Jesus never repudiated his people

Nowhere in the New Testament can an authentic word of Jesus be found to substantiate either the so-called "Jewish rejection of Christ," or its equally unscriptural corollary, "the rejection of Israel by Jesus."

Many church fathers attempt to make up for this "deficiency" in one of three ways. Some make Paul bear the brunt of it. Chrysostom, for example, declares, " 'If any one has no love for the Lord, let him be accursed' (1 Cor. 16:22). . . . It is not I but Paul who has cursed them [the Jews], indeed not even Paul, but Christ, who speaks through him."[1]

Others, such as Isidore of Seville, attribute to Jesus that which they themselves want to be true: "The Jews are being punished because of the crimes they have committed against Jesus. . . . He himself [Jesus] has called the Gentiles and rejected the Jews."[2] Since "the Jews" murdered "the Son of God," God must reject, disperse, and punish them forever. Both the destruction of the temple and their dispersion bear witness to their "deicide." This train of thought cuts across all the writings of the early Christian church fathers, and is often accompanied by the obviously malicious delight of the authors.[3]

The third method of substantiating Israel's rejection has lost none of its popularity from the time of the evangelists through the church fathers and into our own century. In this case the prophets of Israel are quoted against their own people. "Hear, O heavens, and give ear, O earth; for the Lord has spoken: 'Sons have I reared and brought up, but they have rebelled against me. The ox knows its owner, and the ass its master's crib; but Israel does not know, my people does not understand' " (Isa. 1:2ff.). This "defection" of Israel was tangibly illustrated by placing an ox and an ass in the stable at Bethlehem to demonstrate typologically as well as iconographically that, by contrast with the Jews, such animals "recognized" the child in the manger as the future Savior.

"The house of Israel and the house of Judah have broken my covenant which I made with their fathers. Therefore . . . I am bringing evil upon them which they cannot escape," rails Jeremiah (11:10f.) in the name of his Lord. "I will send sword, famine, and pestilence upon them, until they shall be utterly destroyed from the land" (Jer. 24:10).

Isaiah accuses his city, Jerusalem, of having "become a harlot" (Isa. 1:21). Jeremiah calls her "a widow . . . because the Lord has made her suffer for the multitude of her transgressions" (Jer. 1:1-5). Ezekiel speaks of her as a "blood city" because of her "abominable deeds," "guilty of the blood" that she has shed and "defiled by idols," and pronounces God's judgment upon her: "Therefore I have made you a reproach to the nations, and a mocking to all the countries" (Ezek. 22:2ff.).

That all of these reproofs issued by the great prophets reflected their impassioned, though injured love for Israel and that in the end everything they said was nothing but relentless self-criticism, was soon forgotten by the early church. Instead, all these warnings were transformed into tirades of hatred which served to legitimize the "rejection of Israel" as coming from God, and to enlist Christian cooperation in the actualizing of these warnings as a God-pleasing act of faith.

In the process of translating the Hebrew term *navi* into the Greek "prophet" it was also forgotten that these great admonishers of Israel were not predictors or foretellers of divine providence and that they actually embodied the divinely inspired voice of the national conscience. In all of their visions they constantly confronted the people with moral and religious alternatives, saying in effect, "Disaster and ruin will be your lot if you depart from the teachings of God; but happiness and blessing await you if you walk in God's ways."

Not least, it was forgotten or intentionally overlooked that in Israel all prophecy was composed of three parts: a reminder of covenant responsibilities followed by explicit and disturbing threats, concluding invariably with words of consolation, encouragement, comfort, and the promise of divine forgiveness.

By taking the warnings of disaster out of their prophetic context in order to attribute them to Jesus, or to appeal to them as the irrevocable judgments of God, the evangelists transformed the God of love into an avenging demon, degraded God's people to unbelieving "children of the devil," and distorted the joyful message of salvation for the Gentiles into a threatening message of disaster for Jesus' natural brothers and sisters.

Were those in the church who dared to doubt the faithfulness of a God whose mercy always triumphs over the sin of Israel not aware that by doing so they were placing their own future salvation in question?

According to the New Testament the church became a "shoot" of Israel grafted into the original stem of the olive tree (Rom. 11:16ff.) in order that the Gentiles might become "fellow heirs," "fellow citizens with the saints," and "partakers of the promise" (Eph. 2:11—3:6)—but in no way the sole possessors of a permanent covenant with God "for all time." According to both Testaments, only the natural people of Israel are entitled to such a covenant.[4]

Is then the church immune to its own theory of reprisal which, in contradiction to the teaching of Jesus (Matt. 5:44ff.; Luke 6:35ff.), reduces the God of Israel to a paymaster who repays like with like—who responds to human unfaithfulness by terminating his covenant? If "all the promises of God find their Yes" in Jesus (2 Cor. 1:20), and "the gifts and the call of God are irrevocable" (Rom 11:29), surely the Christian faith cannot be based on a breach in divine fidelity to the covenant. On the contrary, it must be understood as a consequence of God's fidelity to the covenant which, ever since Abraham, includes "all the families of the earth" (Gen. 12:3) in the blessing of God. "God is faithful" (2 Cor. 1:18). This word of Paul must be considered equally valid for both Testaments, all the more since it is also Paul who proclaims that "all Israel will be saved" (Rom. 11:25ff.). Is it not time to begin thinking in this way?

Unfortunately, even in our day there is no lack of Christian "punitive theologians" who seem to know the will of God perfectly:

> The burden of God, the burden of guilt, the burden of God's wrath, the burden of unspeakable suffering, the burden of the world . . . rest upon him [Israel].[5]

> The judgment [of Israel] began with the fall of Jerusalem and continues throughout human history. . . . The people who stand under the judgment of God cannot live and dare not die. . . .[6]

> Jesus is the Messiah promised by the Old Testament; the chosen people, however, rejected him and the result was their exclusion from the history of salvation.[7]

From Jesus himself we hear nothing of such unloving "condemnation of Israel," its "expulsion," its "rejection," or its "fall." Nor do we hear of any "curse," which is said to have led to Israel's replacement by the Gentile church as the people of God.[8] Such notions are diametrically opposed to everything he stood for during his earthly life.

"You shall call his name Jesus, for he will save his people from their sins" (Matt. 1:21). This was said before his birth; and until his death—which he suffered on behalf of his people as "King of the Jews"—all of his striving, preaching, exhortation, and attempts at conversion were intended solely for the sake of the well-being and salvation of his own people, the Jews.

Similarly, he chose 12 disciples to make it clear that he, like the prophets before him, considered Israel as a totality and was not willing to abandon either the lost tribes or the "lost sheep of the house of Israel."

His confession of "the God of Abraham, and the God of Isaac, and the God of Jacob" (Mark 12:26f.), as the Creator of the world is called in almost all Jewish prayers, is equally informative. Twice he emphasizes the advantage which, in his opinion, is accorded those who are descendants of Abraham (Luke 13:16; 19:9). And for him the creed of Israel is "the greatest commandment" (Mark 12:29).

"Christ became a servant to the circumcised" (Rom. 15:8), Paul later says of the One who came "that he might be revealed to Israel" (John 1:31) and "to confirm the promises given to the patriarchs" (Rom. 15:8)—promises intended primarily for their descendants, the children of Israel. So, in responding to the Samaritan woman who addresses him as "a Jew" (John 4:9), Jesus can declare that "salvation is from the Jews" (John 4:22).

And on four different occasions Jesus repeats his conviction that at least for the time being, this salvation is meant only for the natural children of Israel:

"You are those who have continued with me in my trials," Jesus says to his disciples. "As my Father appointed a kingdom for me, so do I appoint for you that you may eat and drink at my table in my kingdom, and sit on thrones judging the twelve tribes of Israel" (Luke 22:28-30; Matt. 19:28).

The same disciples, at least according to Matthew, are not only forbidden to go to the Gentiles, but even to the Samaritans who were considered half-Jews: "Go nowhere among the Gentiles, and enter no town of the Samaritans, but go rather to the lost sheep of the house of Israel" (Matt. 10:5f.). They, Jesus emphasizes, are the exclusive goal of his mission: "I was sent *only* to the lost sheep of the house of Israel" (Matt. 15:24).

On a third occasion he limits the sphere of his mission nationally when he announces to his disciples: "You will not have gone through all the towns of Israel, before the Son of man comes" (Matt. 10:23).

Jesus responds sharply to the Gentile woman who pleads for the healing of her daughter, in words that at first glance seem almost chauvinistic: "It is not fair to take the children's bread and throw it to the dogs" (Matt. 15:26). Though he characterizes the Gentiles as "dogs" *(kynaria),* later trivialized as "puppies," he affectionately refers to those who are his, as "children."

Yet, he can also say: "Many will come from east and west and sit at table with Abraham, Isaac, and Jacob in the kingdom of heaven, while the sons of the kingdom will be thrown into outer darkness" (Matt. 8:11f.). Among the arguments against the genuineness of this declaration, I shall mention only three. In rabbinic usage the phrase, "Many will come from east and west and sit at table with Abraham," refers to the messianic gathering of Israel from all parts of the world where Jewish people have been scattered—a concept diametrically opposed to the expulsion of Israel mentioned toward the end of the sentence. "Sons of the kingdom" is an expression unknown to Mark and not used in the parallel in Luke (13:28), and which does not occur in rabbinic literature. It is also strange that shortly after the passage in question, the same Jesus can, according to Matthew, praise the "sons of the kingdom" as "good seed" to whom the grace of God is assured (Matt. 13:38).

How strongly and unforgettably Jesus' original sayings must have continued to live in the tradition! The first evangelists could not avoid reporting them, even though they refute as lies all of the later teachings and theories related to "ancient" Israel's disinheritance or displacement.

The first three Gospels, reluctantly and often only in passing, bear witness that Jesus entered the world as the "first-born son" of Mary (Luke 2:7) "in order that he might be the first-born among many brethren" (Rom. 8:29), and that he was by nature a Jew (Rom. 9:5) who lived his entire life "under the law [Torah]" (Gal. 4:4).

Despite all the controversies and debates—indeed, because of his untiring, often impetuous dialogs with scribes and fellow teachers, a method that is to this day still the best rabbinic way of determining truth and interpreting the Bible—Jesus' faithfulness to the Torah in both word and deed remains the best-kept secret in the Synoptics.

In its statement on "The Attitude of Christians toward Jews," issued April 16, 1973, the Conference of Catholic Bishops in France confirms this. "One must not forget that Jesus was born as a Jewish person of his mother Mary and that by his obedience to the Torah and through his prayer he fulfilled his mission within the framework of the covenant people."

Paul, a faithful servant of his Lord, decades later also affirms that such "obedience" is incompatible with the "rejection" of Israelites, when he certifies that "the sonship, the glory, the covenants, the giving of the law, the worship, and the promises" belong to his "brethren," the Israelites (Rom. 9:3-4) as "irrevocable" gifts of God (Rom. 11:29). And, in order to get rid of every last doubt once and for all, he reinforces his position, "I ask, then, has God rejected his people? By no means! . . . God has not rejected his people whom he foreknew" (Rom. 11:1f.).

Given the fact that God himself upholds his election of Israel and Paul specifically acknowledges it, could Jesus possibly have rejected the Jews?

No wonder that Matthew sees in "this most Jewish of Jews," as Joseph Klausner calls Jesus,[9] the embodiment of all Israel: "Out of Egypt I called my son" (Matt. 2:15). This word of Hosea (11:1) symbolizes the exodus and the conquest of the land, both of which recur typologically in the life of Jesus as examples: "Rise, take the child and his mother, and go to the land of Israel. . . . And he arose and took the child and his mother, and went to the land of Israel" (Matt. 2:19ff.). Here the successor of Abraham is called to return to the promised land, as the founding father once was, in obedience to the call of God.

"This is my beloved Son, with whom I am well pleased" (Matt. 3:17). These biblical words are intended to ratify the calling enacted in baptism. Once proclaimed to "my servant, Israel" (Isa. 49:3), they are now directed to the servant of God from Nazareth. When these words of calling are repeated on the Mount of Transfiguration in the presence of two prime witnesses, Moses and Elijah, they call to mind the giving of the law, prophecy, discipleship, and the hope of the last day, all of which are attributed to Jesus as the embodiment of his people. The evangelist in effect declares that Jesus is Israel. Is the embodiment of Israel as a totality a repudiation of God's people? Could Jesus call his fellow Jews "the salt of the earth" (Matt. 5:13), "the light of the world" (Matt. 5:14), "the sons of the kingdom" (Matt. 8:12), those from among whom the righteous are summoned to "eat bread in the kingdom of God" (Luke 14:15ff.)—and yet reject them?

Hans Küng's summary appears to be the best response: "Jesus was a Jew. . . . He was active among Jews and for Jews. His mother Mary, his father Joseph, his family, his followers were Jews. His name was Jewish (Hebrew *Yeshua,* a late form of *Yehoshua,* which means "Yahweh is salvation"). His Bible, his worship, his prayers were Jewish. In the situation at that time he could not have thought of any proclamation among the Gentiles. His message was for the Jewish people, but for this people in its entirety without any exception."[10]

The twofold Jewish command of love was at the core of Jesus' message. Mark tells us: "One of the scribes came up and heard them disputing with one another, and seeing that he [Jesus] answered them well, asked him, 'Which commandment is the first of all?' Jesus answered, 'The first is, "Hear, O Israel: The Lord our God, the Lord is one; and you shall love the Lord your God with all your heart, and with all your soul, and with all your mind, and with all your strength." The second is this, "You shall love your neighbor as yourself." There is no other commandment greater than these' " (Mark 12:28-31).

The ensuing conversation between Jesus and this scribe of the Pharisees is no less enlightening. As expected, the scribe responds by praising Jesus' combination of the two key commands of the Torah (Deut. 6:4-5 and Lev. 19:18), "You are right, Teacher; you have truly said that he is one, and there is no other." He then expresses the essence of the two love commands in his own words. At the conclusion of the passage we read, "When Jesus saw that he answered wisely, he said to him, 'You are not far from the kingdom of God' " (Mark 12:32, 34).

How refreshing this congenial spirit of mutual respect and esteem between two teachers of the Torah sounds! How unlike the alleged animosities between Jesus and the Pharisees, about which we usually hear so much in the Gospels!

Jesus not only tirelessly proclaimed both the love of one's enemies as the ultimate expression of neighborly love, and the selfless love of God; he also provided a living example of such love for those about him:

> He had compassion on them [the throngs of people], because they were like sheep without a shepherd (Mark 6:34).

> The Son of man also came not to be served but to serve (Mark 10:45).

> Love your enemies and pray for those who persecute you, so that you may be sons of your Father who is in heaven (Matt. 5:44f.).
>
> When Peter asked, "Lord, how often shall my brother sin against me, and I forgive him?" Jesus answered, "I do not say to you seven times, but seventy times seven" (Matt. 18:21f.).
>
> Let the children come to me, do not hinder them; for to such belongs the kingdom of God (Mark 10:14).
>
> Of the woman who was a sinner Jesus says, "Her sins, which are many, are forgiven, for she loved much; but he who is forgiven little, loves little" (Luke 7:47f.).
>
> Be merciful, even as your Father is merciful. Judge not, and you will not be judged; condemn not, and you will not be condemned; forgive and you will be forgiven (Luke 6:36f.).
>
> This is my commandment, that you love one another as I have loved you (John 15:12).

Love where love is most necessary—that is the guiding motif and the basic thought of Jesus' ethic. The blessed, whose reward in heaven is great, are the poor, the hungry, the meek, those who mourn, the merciful, those pure in heart, the peacemakers, the persecuted, the reviled, and the oppressed. No one should be angry with or humiliate his neighbor, and the reconciliation of a wronged brother or sister takes precedence over the offering of a gift at the altar.

"Give to him who asks and do not turn from him who wishes to borrow from you. . . . When you give alms do not let your left hand know what your right hand is doing." Whoever does good to "the least of these my brothers," it is as if he had done it to Jesus. The two coins which the widow contributes to the temple treasury are more significant than the great gifts of the rich, for the latter "have given of their abundance, but she out of her poverty. . . ." Only those who know themselves to be free of sin dare throw the first stone at the adulteress. . . .

Joseph Klausner writes, "A man like Jesus, for whom the ethical ideal was everything, was something unheard of in the Judaism of the day." "In his ethical code there is a sublimity, distinctiveness and originality in form unparalleled in any other Hebrew ethical code."[11]

At the pinnacle of his love ethic is the saying about being willing to sacrifice one's self on behalf of others: "Greater love has no man than this, that a man lay down his life for his friends" (John 15:13).

This great word is then followed by his own heroic deed: "This is my blood of the covenant, which is poured out for many" (Mark 14:24). However one wishes to interpret the disputed word "many," the fact that Jesus' sacrificial death was intended for his own covenant people remains indisputable. Thus the original meaning of the words spoken at the Last Supper could have reached beyond the national borders of Israel. Supporting this view is the fact that Jesus expresses the ancient Jewish understanding of vicarious suffering within the framework of covenant thinking. Both Matthew and Mark render the word over the cup, "This is my blood [the blood] of the covenant," whereas Luke and Paul have Jesus say, "This cup is the new covenant in my blood." This leads us to assume that the words, "a new covenant," (which are as characteristic of the Old Testament as is "the covenant") are in all likelihood a later tradition rather than actual words of Jesus. It is God's initial, valid, and irrevocable covenant with the historical people of Israel that Peter has in mind when he addresses his Jewish "brethren" in the temple at Jerusalem after Easter: "You are the sons . . . of the covenant which God gave to your fathers" (Acts 3:25)—an idea Paul also clearly emphasizes (Rom. 9:4).

If Jesus had included non-Jews in his words at the Last Supper or anywhere else, the big "dissension and debate" between Paul and Peter at the apostolic council (Acts 15:2ff.) concerning the Baptism of uncircumcised persons, would remain as incomprehensible as the fact that the mission to the Gentiles was not begun until some 17 years after the Easter experience (Gal. 1:13—2:10).

So we are compelled to conclude that the earliest Christian community, which certainly ought to be the most reliable witness to the teachings of Jesus, was for years of the opinion that the message of the kingdom of God was meant only for the Jews.

Because Jesus' loving compassion and his wish to save were meant for all of his people, especially for the poor, the weak, and sinners, the parochialism, self-interest, and antibiblical quibbling of many of the leaders, particularly the Sadducean overseers of the temple, were bound to awaken his indignation. Usually his moral outrage was directed against "a Pharisee" (Luke 7:36; 18:10), "the Pharisee" (Luke 7:39), or "some of the Pharisees" (Luke 19:39). These individual cases, no less typical of the Talmud,[12] in the Greek Gospels were soon generalized to "the Pharisees," or "all of the Pharisees." In the Johannine text this generalization became universal in scope, "the Jews."

Evidence for Jesus' solidarity with his people is provided by his "laments" and "reproaches," which testify eloquently to his fiery temperament, his vivid use of imagery, and his passionate love for Israel—exactly like the prophets before him. Isaiah also publicly denounced the leaders of Israel:

> The Lord enters into judgment with the elders and princes of

> his people: "It is you who have devoured the vineyard, the spoil of the poor is in your houses. What do you mean by crushing my people, by grinding the face of the poor?" says the Lord God of hosts (Isa. 3:14-15).

> Ho, shepherds of Israel who have been feeding yourselves [declares Ezekiel, accusing the same elite of the people], You eat the fat, you clothe yourselves with the wool, you slaughter the fatlings; but you do not feed the sheep. . . . Therefore, you shepherds, hear the word of the Lord. . . . Behold, I am against the shepherds; and I will require my sheep at their hand. . . . I will rescue my sheep from their mouths, that they may not be food for them (Ezek. 34:2ff.).

Malachi thunders in the name of his Lord against the predecessors of the same Sadducees whom Jesus reprimands: "And now, O priests, this command is for you. If you will not listen, if you will not lay it to heart to give glory to my name . . . then I will send the curse upon you and I will curse your blessings; indeed I have already cursed them, because you do not lay it to heart" (Mal. 2:1-2).

Later the reproaches of Jesus are directed against the same city, the abuses of its priests, and the lack of protection for its "children": "O Jerusalem, Jerusalem, killing the prophets and stoning those who are sent to you! How often would I have gathered your children together as a hen gathers her brood under her wings, and you would not!" (Matt. 23:37).

Do not the laments of Jesus sound loving and reserved by comparison with the reprimands and threatened curses of the prophets? Yet their common concern is one and the same: a call to repentance issued to the people, a holy anger directed against the wicked shepherds who feed themselves, and above all, a deep longing for the salvation and welfare of Israel.

Jesus' teaching as a whole and his preaching which he "always taught in synagogues and in the temple, where all Jews come together" (John 18:20), are permeated with this all-embracing love for his people—a love which knows as little about a rejection of Israel as it knows about a replacement of Israel by the Gentiles.

Since no authentic words of Jesus imply the repudiation of Israel, only the parables remained, into or out of which the rejection-theologians of the Gentile church would later read either the "hardening" or the "expulsion" of Israel.

Joachim Jeremias has demonstrated "the story of the centuries of distortion and ill-usage which the parables have suffered through allegorical interpretation,"[13] so that "the parables confront us with a difficult problem, namely, the recovery of their original meaning."[14] The reason for this is that "already in the earliest period of all, during the first decade after the death of Jesus, the parables had undergone a certain amount of reinterpretation."[15] Belonging to this "reinterpretation," as Jeremias explains in the following pages, are erroneous translations from the original Semitic texts, resulting in "innumerable alterations in their meaning";[16] "embellishments" such as "stylistic expedients" and the "insertion . . . of words";[17] "a shift of emphasis";[18] "the fusion of two parables into one";[19] indications of "situations which have been deduced from the content of the parables and . . . found to be secondary";[20] and, not least, "very often an existing interpretation has been modified or expanded."[21]

All of this should be taken into account when we focus our attention on the favorite parable of those who advocate the "displacement theory," namely, the parable of the wicked vinedressers (Mark 12:1-12; Matt. 21:33-46; Luke 20:9-19), from which the early church fathers already inferred that since the "unbelieving Jews" had been rejected, the Gentile church had, through Jesus Christ, inherited Israel's place as the "new people of God." This view is still held today. Leonhard Goppelt, for example, writes:

> In the Jews' rejection of Him, Jesus saw . . . the consistent conclusion of the conflict between God and Israel that had existed ever since the establishment of their covenant relationship. . . . Consequently, after His rejection the Lord of the vineyard would "come and destroy the tenants, and give the vineyard to others" (Mk 12.9 par.). This sentence . . . announced . . . that what the prophets had threatened was now taking place in redemptive history, namely, the covenant people as such were being rejected.[22]

First let us look at the text according to Matthew. Jesus is speaking to the high priests and elders in the temple:

> Hear another parable. There was a householder who planted a vineyard, and set a hedge around it, and dug a winepress in it, and built a tower, and let it out to tenants, and went into another country. When the season of fruit drew near, he sent his servants to the tenants, to get his fruit; and the tenants took his servants and beat one, killed another, and stoned another. Again he sent other servants, more than the first; and they did the same to them. Afterwards he sent his son to them, saying, "They will respect my son." But when the tenants saw the son, they said to themselves, "This is the heir; come, let us kill him and have his inheritance." And they took him and cast him out of the vineyard, and killed him. When therefore the owner of the vineyard comes, what will he do to those tenants? They said to him, "He will put those wretches to a miserable death, and let out the vineyard to other tenants who will give him the fruits in their season."

> Jesus said to them, "Have you never read in the scriptures:
> 'The very stone which the builders rejected
> has become the head of the corner;
> this was the Lord's doing,
> and it is marvelous in our eyes'?
> Therefore I tell you, the kingdom of God will be taken away from you and given to a nation producing the fruits of it."
>
> When the chief priests and the Pharisees heard his parables, they perceived that he was speaking about them. But when they tried to arrest him, they feared the multitudes, because they held him to be a prophet (Matt. 21:33-46).

What is the meaning of this parable? The *Jerusalem Bible* explains it in a note: "The proprietor is God; the vineyard the Chosen People, Israel . . . the servants the prophets; the son Jesus, put to death outside the walls of Jerusalem; the murderous farmers the faithless Jews; the nation to which the vineyard will be entrusted, the pagans."[23]

The Catholic New Testament scholar Josef Schmidt asserts that this parable "contains a type of historical theology which contemplates the guilt of Israel throughout its entire history. The greatest measure of guilt, however, is borne by the contemporary generation to which Jesus speaks, because it delivered the 'beloved son' to death. With that, God's patience is exhausted. The result is Israel's rejection. In its place a new, spiritual Israel is called and established by God from among the Gentiles. 'The people' who are to assume the inheritance of the Jews is a reference to the church."[24]

"The parable is so transparent," writes Wolfgang Trilling, "that it can only be understood of the disloyal people of Israel. They refused to listen to God's envoys and hardened their hearts."[25]

This is, in fact, how Matthew understands it, for, as Franz

Mussner emphasizes, he is the evangelist in whose account "the anti-Jewish tendency . . . is most apparent."[26] So it is not at all surprising that the sharpest anti-Jewish word of the parable is found only in Matthew: "Therefore I tell you, the kingdom of God will be taken away from you and given to a nation producing the fruits of it" (Matt. 21:43). This statement cannot be attributed to Jesus himself because:

1. It does not fit the poetic imagery which characterizes this and the other parables of Jesus. Instead it departs abruptly from prophetic speech to inform the rulers of the temple—prosaically, tersely, and succinctly—of their rejection and displacement.

2. The "you" is addressed to the leaders of Israel who are present; not to a "people" from whom something can be taken and given to a more able "people."

3. Wedged as it is between a compound quotation which sets forth the main point of the parable (Matt. 21:42) and the natural conclusion (Matt. 21:44), which reports the effect of the parable on its intended hearers, this verse destroys the logical continuity of the passage.

4. Nowhere in the teaching of Jesus is the kingdom of God depicted as a thing that can be possessed, or as a commodity that can be passed from one person or people to another. Its "incomprehensibility" is the principal assertion Jesus makes about the kingly rule of God.

Moreover, when we realize that this pronouncement of rejection is not found in the parallels in Mark and Luke—that it is indeed unique to Matthew—we understand how W. Trilling can "for compositional, stylistic, and practical reasons," conclude that verse 43 in its entirety "has definitely been composed by Matthew."[27] "Matthew," says J. Jeremias, "pursued the allegorizing method consistently to the end."[28]

But what is the original meaning of the parable for Jesus himself? Was he speaking of the rejection of the people of Israel? By no means! Ever since Isaiah 5 the vineyard has been a classical image of Israel as God's planting.[29] In Jesus' parable it is not the vineyard that opposes God's plan, abuses his messengers, and kills his son, but the vinedressers, who without a doubt represent the leaders of Israel who had been appointed to care for God's people on his behalf, like good tenants. It is to them that the parable is directed; they are the target of Jesus' attack. It is told "against them," as Mark 12:12 and Luke 20:19 put it—and according to all three Synoptics the leaders feel themselves personally addressed: "When the chief priests and the Pharisees heard his parables, they perceived that he was speaking about them" (Matt. 21:45).

Franz Mussner also concludes: "This parable as originally spoken by Jesus was most likely a warning to the spiritual leaders of Israel at the time."[30] J. Jeremias goes further, in that he questions the originality of the reference to Isaiah 5, since it is not the original Hebrew text that is used, but a Greek translation (the Septuagint).[31] He also finds equating the "son" in the parable with Jesus himself equally questionable, "for the mass of his hearers the Messianic significance of the son could not be taken for granted, since no evidence is forthcoming for the application of the title 'Son of God' to the Messiah in pre-Christian Palestinian Judaism."[32] In this he concurs with W. G. Kümmel, whom he cites: "No Jew, hearing in our parable the story of the mission and slaying of the 'son,' could have dreamed of applying it to the sending of the Messiah."[33]

After peeling away several layers of subsequent editorial glosses, Jeremias comes to the conclusion that Jesus originally spoke without allegory about "the revolutionary attitude of the

Galilean peasants towards the foreign landlords," in other words, about real tenants who would have been willing to kill the son and rightful heir in order to obtain the owner's vineyard "as unclaimed property." With this in mind, Jeremias attempts to recapture the original intent of the parable in the following words: "Like so many other parables of Jesus, it vindicates the offer of the gospel to the poor. You, it says, you tenants of the vineyard, you leaders of the people! you have opposed, have multiplied rebellion against God. Your cup is full! Therefore shall the vineyard of God be given to 'others' " whom "we must . . . interpret . . . as the {poor}."[34]

Whatever the case may be, Jesus' parable is a parable of admonition concerned with internal Jewish matters, and intended to serve the welfare of his own people, Israel.

The parables of the barren fig tree, the two sons, the narrow gate, the lost son, and the laborers in the vineyard all experienced a similar fate; they were all twisted and distorted until they were made to affirm—or at least suggest—that which their originator would have considered blasphemy during his lifetime: the rejection of the chosen, covenant people of God.

But didn't Jesus say he wanted to destroy the temple? Three of the evangelists hold a different opinion. Mark does mention that some witnesses testified, "We heard him say, 'I will destroy this temple that is made with hands, and in three days I will build another, not made with hands' " (Mark 14:58), but he emphasizes that they "bore false witness" (Mark 14:57), and he adds, "not even so did their testimony agree" (Mark 14:59). Matthew also labels as "false witness" the testimony of the two who came forward and said, "This fellow said, 'I am able to destroy the temple of God, and to build it in three days' " (Matt. 26:61). In the face of this false accusation Jesus rightfully remained silent, and the high priest rightfully moved on to the next point on the agenda (Matt. 26:62f.).

John says nothing at all about Jesus' destroying the temple, but instead focuses on its reconstruction. Speaking to "the Jews" Jesus declares, "Destroy this temple, and in three days I will raise it up" (John 2:19). And then, to avoid the slightest suspicion about the temple's destruction, John interprets the saying Christologically, "But he [Jesus] spoke of the temple of his body" (John 2:21), thereby transferring these words into the nebulous realm of allegory.

Still more convincing is the absence of any criticism by Jesus of the temple cult itself. Instead we find a whole string of sayings of Jesus that approve of the sacrificial offerings in Jerusalem:

> So if you are offering your gift at the altar, and there remember that your brother has something against you, leave your gift there before the altar and go; first be reconciled to your brother, and then come and offer your gift (Matt. 5:23-24).
>
> Go, show yourself to the priest, and offer for your cleansing what Moses commanded, for a proof to them [Jesus charges the healed leper] (Mark 1:44).
>
> Every sacrifice will be salted with salt (Mark 9:49).[35]

Still Jesus, who "went to the synagogue, as his custom was, on the sabbath day" (Luke 4:15), also drove the shopkeepers from the temple:

> And he entered the temple and began to drive out those who sold and those who bought in the temple, and he overturned the tables of the money changers and the seats of those who

> sold pigeons. . . . And he taught, and said to them, "Is it not written, 'My house shall be called a house of prayer for the nations?' But you have made it a den of robbers" (Mark 11:15-17).

Jesus here not only quotes Isa. 56:7 and Jer. 7:11 but also carries out the pious wish of a third prophet, "And there shall no longer be a trader in the house of the Lord of hosts on that day" (Zech. 14:21).

His second, apparently no less forceful, cleansing of the temple, is also significant: "And he would not allow any one to carry anything through the temple" (Mark 11:16)—which corresponds exactly to the instructions of the Mishnah:[36] "He may not enter the Temple Mount with his staff or his sandal or his wallet, or with the dust upon his feet, nor may he make of it a short by-path . . ." (m.Ber. 9:5).

The words that most strikingly describe Jesus' reverence for the temple come from Ps. 69:10 and are quoted by his disciples, who were no less impressed by the righteous anger of Jesus' cleansing than readers of today: "Zeal for thy house will consume me" (John 2:17). This same "consuming zeal" for the purity of the temple worship is also expressed in Jesus' conflict with the "Pharisees":

> Woe to you, blind guides, who say, "If any one swears by the temple, it is nothing; but if one swears by the gold of the temple, he is bound by his oath" . . . . Which is greater, the gold or the temple that has made the gold sacred? (Matt. 23:16-17).

Finally, already as a young boy Jesus says to his parents in the temple: "How is it that you sought me? Did you not know that I must be in that which is my Father's?" (Luke 2:49; author's trans.). The clearest interpretations relate these words to the claim that the temple is the "house of God," as it has always been called in Jewish literature.

Why should Jesus have foretold the destruction of the temple? "As for these things which you see, the days will come when there shall not be left here one stone upon another that will not be thrown down" (Luke 21:6). This statement in all the Synoptics is a part of the well-known "Lament over Jerusalem," and simply proves, as Rabbi Leo Baeck has demonstrated, that the Gospels were not written until after the destruction of Jerusalem in the year 70. Concerning Jesus' last and crowning lament regarding the scribes, ". . . that upon you may come all the righteous blood shed on earth, from the blood of innocent Abel to the blood of Zechariah the son of Barachiah, whom you murdered between the sanctuary and the altar" (Matt. 23:35), Leo Baeck writes: "Since it is said of Zechariah [by Josephus, *War* 4,5,4] . . . that in the year 68 the Zealots stabbed him to death between the sanctuary and the altar—the exact spot where Matthew fixes the deed—the time to which this lament and woe belongs is made clear. It could not have been spoken by Jesus but has been put in his mouth. It originated in the Christian community that experienced the destruction of the temple and saw in it a great sign."[37]

The same thing can be said about other "laments over Jerusalem" and the allusions to the destruction of the temple, which have the unmistakable aftertaste of a *vaticinium ex eventu* ("prophecy after the event")—as the philosopher Celsus already said in the second century after Christ: It did not happen because it was foretold, but rather it was foretold because it had already happened.

In addition it should be said that no biblically informed Jew would have accused other Jews of Abel's murder because Noah's sacrifice (Gen. 8:20) absolved all postflood humanity. So not even a Gentile can be made responsible for Cain's sins—let alone Israel, whose history first begins with Abraham.[38]

And yet we know of a similar temple word, from the mouth of a later contemporary of Jesus, who is considered one of the fathers of the Mishnah. Rabbi Jochanan ben Zakkai directed his attacks against militant messianists, just as Jesus had against the Zealots[39] who were determined to support God's plan of salvation with weapons. "If young men say to you: Let us go and build the temple, do not listen to them, but if the old men say to you: Come and let us tear down the temple, do as they say. For the building up of young men is a tearing down and the tearing down of old men is a building up. The proof of this is Rehoboam, the son of Solomon."[40] Along with many exegetes I am of the opinion that both temple words are from the year A.D. 70, when the temple was destroyed or soon thereafter.

That Jesus was not willing to condemn those in Israel who despised him gives credence not only to his command to love one's enemies, but also to the saying, "Whoever says a word against the Son of man will be forgiven" (Matt. 12:32). In a similar way he also extended his love to those Jews who did not want to receive him, for "the Son of man is not come to condemn, but to save." And shortly thereafter, he says even more clearly, "the Son of man came to seek and to save the lost" (Luke 19:10).

There is no single anti-Jewish statement or parable in the entire New Testament which does not stand in crass contradiction to the overall picture of this Jewish man of God, whose living expression of the message of love condemns all textual lovelessness as a lie.

That's all well and good, some readers may now interject, but because of their guilt for the crucifixion the Jews have still forfeited their calling and have been rejected by Jesus. My response is: the word from the cross of Golgotha is closer to demonstrating the opposite: "Father, forgive them, for they know not what they do!" (Luke 23:34).

Doesn't this petition sound like the crowning expression of selfless love, a love which is willing even to pray for one's tormenters? And isn't it characteristic of a certain demonic spirit within the Gentile church that later copyists of the Greek Gospels left out this key sentence, obviously because it sounded too charitable, perhaps even pro-Jewish—despite the fact that not one iota of the wording points to the Jews?

And isn't it just as true that the resurrected one appeared solely to the Jews, and that all of the witnesses of the Easter event were without exception sons and daughters of Israel? In order to remove all doubt concerning the meaning of the resurrection, Peter, as head of the earliest church, says to his Jewish "brethren" in Jerusalem: "God, having raised up his servant, sent him to you first, to bless you" (Acts 3:26).

The intention of Jesus after Easter remained the same as it was before Easter: dedication, care, and devotion for Israel.

One last word concerning the church's teaching of salvation. If Jesus has died "for us all" (Rom. 8:32), and if through "the blood of his cross" everything, "whether on earth or in heaven" has been reconciled to God (Col. 1:20), how can one restrict his sacrificial death to an exclusive possession of the church? Did he die for everyone *except* his own beloved people, Israel, for whom his entire earthly life and mission were intended?

Where is that written? How could this Rabbi Jesus, whose

love for all of Israel—including its sinners, apostates, and lost sheep—speak so persuasively in each of his words and deeds, offer salvation to the Gentile world only to repudiate his own flesh and blood?

When and where did he ever say that? And if he didn't, then who assumes the authority to hate, where he loved; to punish, where he forgave; to reject, where he came only to heal and to bless? Can anyone hold that he or she is a follower of Christ without demonstrating the same active sympathy for the physical brothers and sisters of the Nazarene that permeated Jesus' entire work on earth?

The Christian-Jewish dialog, which has in our day finally begun to be truly candid, expects answers to these questions of conscience.

Prolog for tomorrow

If the concept "Messiah" is essentially so Jewish that it has been introduced into all of the languages of Europe as a borrowed Hebrew word, if messianism, in the sense of a theopolitical longing for salvation, has prevailed for over two centuries as a sort of feverish Jewish illness, and if Jesus of Narareth lived his entire earthly life among a people whose world of thought was marked by an acute expectation of the messianic age, why is it that the Jews, of all people, do not recognize him as the Messiah?

The Jewish answer is: because he was not the Messiah of Israel, although he became the Savior of the church. Neither of these conclusions needs to be verified theologically. For Jews, the undeniably unredeemed state of the world—which the militant anti-Judaism of so many Christians all too painfully underscores—is enough to confirm the "not yet" of all expectations of salvation.

Christians, on the other hand, waive every attempt to substantiate their faith. They readily admit that the search for the historical Jesus is encumbered with uncertainties and questionable elements, and maintain that revelation is not a purely historical fact but instead occurs as an event of faith. It is easy to point out the abundant contradictions and inconsistencies that were already attributed to the earthly Jesus in the Greek Gospels. But do they not also demonstrate the depth of the multilayered impression which he left on the hearts of his disciples?

It is true: as a Jew among Jews, Jesus was not unique. As teachers of Torah and interpreters of Scripture, other rabbis also contributed their special insights and ideas to the overall wisdom of Israel. Thousands of his fellow Jews died as religious heroes and martyrs on Roman crosses like the one on which he lost his life. As messianic prophets, others called for repentance in the face of the new age which was expected to dawn any day. And more than a dozen messianic contenders were crucified.

Even the debate about Jesus' messiahship within Judaism after Golgotha was not exceptional. Whereas his suffering and ignominious death became proof of his failure for some, for others the same passion became a clear indication that God had accepted his self-sacrifice.

It is equally true that only in the case of the Nazarene did his disciples experience him as the resurrected One; and as a result, that he would return as Messiah became the certainty of their existence. It is no less true, moreover, that this certainty soon crossed the borders of Israel to become the certainty of salvation which called innumerable Gentiles away from their idols to the living God of Abraham, Isaac, and Jacob.

Last but not least, it is an indisputable fact that Jesus of Nazareth—and he alone—became a person of vital significance for millions of believing Christians whom he has helped, and continues to help, to a better life, an undying hope, and a peaceful death.

If the Hebrew good news of the boundless love of God, which Isaiah calls "salvation" (Isa. 49:6), would have reached the four corners of the world in the name of a Greek philosopher or a Roman orator, most Jews would have had serious misgivings. But since this spread of monotheism throughout the Western world was accomplished in the name of a pious, God-fearing Jew, the story of its influence cannot remain irrelevant for Israel.

Granted, some of the more open-minded will now ask whether the figure on the church's crucifixes is actually still identical with the man from Galilee. How did the believing Nazarene become the Savior in whom others believed, the proclaimer become the proclaimed, the earthly Son of man become the heavenly Son of God, the preacher of the Sermon on the Mount the bringer of salvation? In short, how did the Jesus of history become the Christ of faith?

Certainly the proliferation of legends, the free rendering of texts, and the process of mythologizing have played a significant role in exalting the humble Nazarene; and yet, after discounting all Hellenization and foreign elements, we are left with an irreducible residue that resists demythologizing. "A certain something," Martin Buber calls it, for which Jesus deserves "a great place . . . in Israel's history of faith"; a place that "cannot be described by any of the usual categories"—which in the end can be understood as an acknowledgment of the "mystery of Jesus."

Son of God, Redeemer, Son of David, Lord, Master, Servant of God, and a dozen other titles, which only a few in Israel took literally, are basically nothing more than the spontaneous attempts of the reticent rural folk of Galilee to give expression to their amazement. They simply wanted to express verbally that they believed him, that they regarded him as a person of faith, that they were willing to learn to trust in God—blindly and without question, as he did.

A generation later, far from Jesus' homeland, in a totally different religious environment, this confusing polyphony gave rise to a theology which placed its faith in him, intensified Jewish enthusiasm to the point of Greek veneration, and eventually exalted him to Savior of the world.

Did the initial community believe too little? Or did his later disciples believe too much? Who recognized him? Who mistook him? Or was it faith (Eph. 3:17) that after Easter transformed him into something he had never been, nor could have been?

Any Jewish scholar who examines the New Testament will find that Jesus was undoubtedly a Jew—not just a marginal Jew, nor a lukewarm, *pro forma* Jew, but a true Jew, whose spiritual roots rose out of the prophetic core of Israel's faith, that he was closely related to the Pharisees, that he was a Galilean, and that, on top of everything else, he was a master in the art of telling parables. But to maintain that he was only a Jew, or only a Pharisee, or nothing but a wandering preacher, would be the height of unbiblical arrogance. Moreover, it would contradict one of the basic principles of those same Pharisees, which asserts that negative testimony is not allowed. In Israel no one can state before a court what an accused person has *not* said, or done, or been involved in. There is just as little ground for anyone today to testify who Jesus was not. Using the sources at our disposal we can attempt to determine who Jesus was, what he accomplished, and which sayings were most likely his. But what he became after Easter Sunday for believing Jewish Christians and later for the Gentile church in addition to and beyond this remains an untouchable prerogative of faith that belongs to the mystery of the church.

"I do not know"—this is the only honest reply a Jew can give to the Christology of the church. In this instance no presumptuous attempt to unveil the mystery in a premature and purely rational way will serve the truth.

Of this, however, I am certain: the mission mandate which the prophets issued to Israel was clear. She was to be a light to the nations. "I am the Lord, I have called you in righteousness, I have taken you by the hand and kept you; I have given you as a covenant to the people, a light to the nations" (Isa. 42:6), declares the book of Isaiah. And shortly thereafter it states the message of God even more clearly:

> It is too light a thing that you should be my servant to raise up the tribes of Jacob and to restore the preserved of Israel; I will give you as a light to the nations, that my salvation may reach to the end of the earth (Isa. 49:6).

For Judaism this being a light to all the peoples of the world means bearing witness, most often silently, by the example of one's actions, but also in suffering for God's omnipotence and his inexhaustible love. It does not presume to convert Gentiles to Judaism. Rather, it allows God alone to determine when and where Israel's service on behalf of mankind will bear fruit.

The mandate has always meant leading Gentiles to the one God, but not taking them into the synagogue. For this reason we have for centuries fully acknowledged the validity of other ways of salvation. It is our mission to proclaim monotheism, not Judaism. "Salvation is from the Jews" (John 4:22), says the Johannine Jesus. It comes *from* Israel in order that it might go out *to* all peoples. It was preached and promised by the prophets; it has been largely accomplished in the name of Jesus of Nazareth. So he must certainly have been more than the son of a Galilean carpenter who merely called into being a movement of repentance. What this *more* was, I don't know. The sages of the Talmud teach us that every person is unique. Every human being conceals a mystery within himself or herself that none of his or her brothers and sisters is able to uncover completely.

Franz Rosenzweig affirms the statement of the Johannine Jesus, "No one comes to the Father, but by me" (John 14:6)—no one, unless he or she is already with the Father—and precisely this is true of Israel, "which walks in the light of God's countenance without a mediator."[1] The fear of standing alone before God was also not unknown in Israel. "I stood between the Lord and you at that time, to declare to you the word of the Lord," says Moses, the great mediator, "For you were afraid because of the fire [of God], and you did not go up into the mountain" (Deut. 5:5).

The Gentile world at Jesus' time was crowded with divine men, sons of gods, and demi-gods, whose task it was to mediate between heaven and earth. God's pedagogy, as the medieval Jewish scholar Maimonides taught, made use of trusted thought-patterns and traditional practices gradually to lead humanity to higher insights.

Is it not conceivable that this pedagogy should enable the post-Easter Nazarene to become in all places the recognized mediator (in Greek dress) in order through him "to eradicate idolatry in the Gentile world" and by means of the exalted

Christ "to bring the knowledge of God to the farthest islands?"[2] Or is the Christology of the church a misguided false teaching? Are there false teachings that can last for millenia and conjure up worldwide faith communities? Can a church that is able to "move mountains" in the name of God be founded on illusions? Can false teachers and deluded persons submit to torture and persecution—to the point of joyful martyrdom *ad majorem Dei gloriam?*

An atheist might readily say yes to these questions. As a believing Jew, I cannot attribute a historical development that, despite numerous mistakes and blunders, has carried the message of Israel from Jerusalem into all the world, to the blind coincidence of human errors or to materialistic determinism—though all of these factors may have played a part in furthering the saving purposes of God.

The first hymn in the Protestant hymnal is an ancient hymn of the church, attributed to Bishop Ambrose of the fourth century: *Veni, redemptor gentium!* Martin Luther translated it into the German, *"Nun komm, der Heiden Heiland!"* ("Savior of the Nations, Come") in the year 1524. I believe that both Ambrose and Luther are right. Jesus of Nazareth has become, in the inscrutable ways of God, the Savior of the Gentiles.

It doesn't take theology to establish this. A sympathetic understanding is sufficient to recognize the certainty of faith evidenced by the unselfish way in which true Christians willingly sacrifice their bodies and souls. One doesn't argue over a faith that is lived out, thought through, and willing to suffer. The outer shell of the church's Christology may be thick and gnarled, but the inner kernel that determines its nature and lends it radiance is Jesus, the Jew from Nazareth.

Can he who parted the Red Sea to save all Israel not call a pious Jew to be Savior of the Gentiles? If the Persian King

Cyrus can be spoken of as the "anointed" of the Lord (Isa. 45:1), because he, as God's instrument, made possible the return of the Jews to their biblical home, why can a rabbi from Nazareth not be designated Savior of the nations—as redeemer from idolatry and faithlessness so that "he might bring . . . to God" (1 Peter 3:18) those "having no hope and without God in the world" (Eph. 2:12) so that "through him [they] have confidence in God" (1 Peter 1:21)?

"Behold, I am the Lord, the God of all flesh; is anything too hard for me?" declares the Creator (Jer. 32:27).

Finally, it is the basic idea of Christology that human suffering, weakness, and tragic defeat are not the last things that can be said about our life. They need not be accepted as indications of failures, but can be experienced as demonstrations of God's grace which lead to a higher life, beyond the grave and nearer to God. Basically, every Christian hopes to be allowed to share Jesus' destiny: to pass through suffering and death, from which no mortal is spared, to resurrection and eternal life. Since the time of the Maccabees this same conviction is also one of the cornerstones of Jewish faith.

The rejection of all premature offers of apparent salvation by the Jews is nothing other than a persistent "yes" to the prophetic promise of the salvation that is to come, and a mighty "yea and Amen" to the kingdom of God on earth which Jesus, along with all believing Jews, so longingly awaited.

Jews and Christians are called to preserve and demonstrate this messianic hope for all the world. In the words of Hans-Werner Bartsch: "The question concerning the right relationship between Jews and Christians is not whether Israel wishes to accept Christ as its Messiah, but rather the opposite, whether Christendom will acknowledge that it has been accepted by grace into the covenant between God and Israel. It is Christendom that should be asked by Israel whether it wishes to share in Israel's hope that God may in the end be everything to everyone (1 Cor. 15:28). . . . As Christians we must allow ourselves to be missionized by Israel, so that we may recapture this hope and from it learn to understand our existence anew."[3]

If faith in the same Father-God, hope in salvation, and knowledge of the God-given meaning of life irrevocably unite us, ought we not seriously ask ourselves where it is that God the Creator separates us, and where *we* prevent or delay our own reconciliation? These questions, which are intended to probe the ultimate meaning of faith in God, belong on the agenda of the true Christian-Jewish dialog which will begin tomorrow.

Part Two

A Christian Perspective

by Ulrich Luz

Introduction

Dear Mr. Lapide:

I have accepted with pleasure the task of responding to your theses on Jesus at the request of the publisher and with your consent because I rejoice at the Jewish-Christian dialog that will result from it. This task has given rise to much that neither of us anticipated when we began: an intensive association, many concentrated conversations, and above all a personal interaction and friendship that I find gratifying and significant. But the task of responding to your work has not been made easier by all of this.

There are two reasons for the difficulty. On the one hand, many of the questions I consider essential topics for a Jewish-Christian discussion concerning Jesus are not raised in your text. I am almost totally in agreement with what you have written in your theses. However, there are many open questions, where we are surely not in agreement and about which we ought to speak. In your text you mention them at best only marginally. On the other hand, upon repeated readings of your manuscript it became increasingly apparent to me that we cannot even begin a dialog at this point. It is not enough that two theologians—a Jew and a Christian—simply begin speaking with one another about Jesus and related themes, even though their personal intentions are honest. We would soon realize that there are *stones lying on the way* which must first be removed, stones on the path of the history between Christians and Jews. Certainly most of us contemporary Christians are not guilty for their being there and can, with good conscience, distance ourselves from them. But we cannot simply overlook the fact *that* they are there. We cannot simply begin a dialog anew in a vacuum. Our position is not indeterminate; rather, we find ourselves at the end of more than 1900 years of Christian-Jewish relations. It is not my intention to begin this letter with a Christian confession of guilt; nor do I think you anticipate such a confession from me. We both know that throughout their history Christians have often confessed their guilt far too zealously. And so I do not wish to speak of guilt in this connection—though in my opinion such guilt exists! Instead I wish to speak of the reality of some 1900 years of mutual history that have contributed to making us what we are. We both know that history holds the possibility of a new beginning, for we both believe in the same God who has the power to forgive sin. Moreover, we both know that this gift of our God does not take place in a vacuum, but here, in the reality of our common history. For this reason beginning anew means clearing away the rubbish that history has piled high, and removing the stones that have accumulated along the way. Rubbish heaps cannot be removed by overlooking them, but by tackling them. Your work on Jesus, if I understand it rightly, has this as its primary purpose.

Accordingly, you could not have left out the first few pages of the introduction. For us Christians they read like a compressed indictment. One of my students who read your manuscript said afterwards, "I was so exasperated that I would not have continued reading the manuscript if we were not going to discuss it." I certainly know that it is not your intention to shout at us, to tell us Christians how bad we have been and are. Rather it is to the *reality* of history that you point. Everything that has been written by theologians, church and council fathers, even by several of the New Testament authors themselves, is there; it cannot be unwritten, even if it displeases us. Such texts continue to have an effect even if we do not like them. We must face this reality even if we disapprove of it and even if we are not personally guilty for it.

With this I come to a point that is very important to me. Just now, I used the words "several of the New Testament authors themselves." Thus I cannot exclude our Christian New Testament from among those factors that have determined the history of your people's suffering within the Christian world. We need but glance at the three principal theses which you refute in the three major segments of the book—that Jesus was the Messiah, that Jesus was rejected by his people, and that Jesus rejected his people. Who makes such claims? The answer must be: not only most Christians in the past, and perhaps some Christians today, but also the New Testament—certainly not the entire New Testament, at least not regarding the second and third theses. For the most part, only statements of individual New Testament authors, and sometimes only single texts, are involved. Nevertheless, these texts exist. I, along with you and with most Christian scholars, am of the opinion that most of these texts—at least in the sense in which we now have them in the New Testament—cannot be traced back to Jesus. Nevertheless, an important problem still remains. Where did these sayings come from? What experiences and thoughts lie behind them? How can they be explained? Perhaps even—what understandable or justifiable concerns do they represent? I make this observation only to indicate that for us Christians the problem is not yet solved when we absolve Jesus of the burden of guilt for the entire tragic development of Christian-Jewish relations; just as little as it is enough to absolve the people of Israel of the guilt of murdering the Messiah or God (which ought to be a foregone conclusion in our day so that one is ashamed even to mention it!).

Having recognized this does not mean that all of the stones have yet been cleared away. Actually it is at this point for us Christians that, in my opinion, the most difficult task first begins. We must critically—not just judgmentally, but critically—come to terms with our New Testament and ask whether and how much it has contributed to the erroneous shifts in emphases so decisive in the history of Jewish-Christian relationships, that is, whether and how much these shifts at least indirectly—and contrary to the intention of the New Testament writers—were determined by it. It is not simply Jesus who is our authority as Christians; rather our authority is the living Jesus Christ to whom the New Testament bears witness. So, Mr. Lapide, though you may conclude not only that the people of Israel should be acquitted from the accusation of having murdered God, but also that Jesus should be acquitted from the accusation of having, at least indirectly, become the instigator of the murder of Jews, for us Christians the case is thereby not yet closed. An acquittal of Jesus is not yet an acquittal of the entire New Testament. There are still a number of dark and difficult passages which we must consider and learn to master precisely because they continue to have an adverse influence. There are still many stones to be cleared out of the way, a task which is primarily ours alone to accomplish as Christians, but not without the help of our Jewish partners in dialog. I speak out in order to avoid any rash attempt to purge the New Testament canon of all anti-Jewish elements. That would be foolish. We cannot simply change the New Testament canon to fit our personal whims; it is as it is. But we surely can learn to read it with different eyes. We can, for example, learn to look at many New Testament passages, particularly when they speak of Jewish guilt, from a perspective that allows us to understand them as pointing to Christian guilt. We can allow just such passages to instruct and correct us, not because they are God's Word but because they are human words. Many stones remain to be cleared away even after the writing of this book.

Now however, in accord with your text, I wish to concentrate on Jesus. First I would like to take up the theses you have advanced concerning Jesus. Then, in conclusion I would like at least to touch upon those questions which to me seem essential for a future Jewish-Christian conversation about Jesus; and in doing so I will also reach beyond the historical figure of Jesus into our present situation, as you did.

Along with you, I am of the opinion that it is difficult, but by no means impossible, to achieve a somewhat accurate picture of the proclamation and the works of Jesus. It is clear that there are trends and biases in the Gospels that become understandable only in the context of the post-Easter communities of the evangelists and their theologies. The tradition involved, like every oral tradition, has undergone a process of development. There are so-called nonauthentic words of Jesus, for example, those that are uttered by early Christian prophets in the name of the exalted Lord Jesus. This means that in many instances the source of a word or tradition concerning Jesus, or its original form must remain uncertain. Like you, I am of the opinion that the great diversity of scholarly hypotheses need not discourage us. There may indeed be too many New Testament scholars in the world, at least by comparison with the number of scholars working in other areas of ancient literature! However, we ought not forget that there is hardly a religious figure of the ancient world about whom we know so much as we know about Jesus. Many a historian who deals with antiquity is envious of the sources at our disposal, the very sources about which we New Testament scholars often complain. Here again I am in complete agreement with you. We need not be so excessively pessimistic and overly distrustful of our sources.

Response to Thesis One

Jesus did not declare himself to his people as Messiah.

I can agree completely with this thesis and even sharpen it. Not only did Jesus not declare himself to his people as the Messiah; more than likely he did not even consider himself to be the Messiah. You didn't say this so directly since it was your primary intention to exonerate Israel from the guilt of having crucified its Messiah. But precisely as a Christian I am interested in the question of how Jesus understood himself, and so must sharpen your first negative thesis a bit.

First let me make two preliminary remarks that I consider essential for a correct understanding.

A. At the time of Jesus Jewish expectations of an eschatological Savior were extremely diverse. You rightly say (p. 29) that the Messiah in some way or another always played a theo-political role. But there were also other expectations which can only be characterized as messianic in a broader sense. They include, for example, the expectations of an eschatological high priest or an eschatological prophet held by several Jewish groups. In particular, there is the expectation of a heavenly "Son of man" which is originally rooted in the Old Testament book of Daniel: "And behold, with the clouds of heaven there came one like a son of man, and he came to the Ancient of Days and was presented before him. And to him was given dominion and glory and kingdom, that all peoples, nations, and languages should serve him" (Dan. 7:13-14).

Influenced by Daniel, several Jewish groups awaited a heavenly figure, whom they called the "Son of man," either as the judge of the world or as a witness or court clerk in the final judgment. The content of such expectations is indirectly rather than directly theo-political in character. When I say that Jesus did not consider himself to be the Messiah, I am for the time being setting aside all of these expectations. At least in connection with the question of the identity of the Son of man, I do not wish to exclude the possibility that Jesus may have considered himself the one whom God would exalt and appoint as the coming Son of man. Even if this were so—which is very uncertain—or if Jesus had at least given his disciples some indication that he believed it to be true, we would still be unable to say that Jesus had revealed himself to Israel as the Messiah and that Israel had become guilty of rejecting its own Messiah. Those who awaited a coming Son of man expected him to be a heavenly figure. No one reckoned that this heavenly person would appear in human form and work in the land of Israel previous to his eschatological appearance. The only one whom some assumed would in the last day be revealed as the Son of man (1 Enoch 70f.) was Enoch, the ancient sage who was taken into heaven by God (Gen. 5:24). If Jesus had considered himself the Son of man in this sense, Israel could not possibly be indicted, for it never understood this claim as messianic. I indicate all of this only to say that for me the thesis that Jesus did not consider himself to be the Messiah does not necessarily predetermine a negative response to the question of Jesus' personal self-understanding. Instead, after we have cleared away the stones we—Jews and Christians together—must inquire into Jesus' own particular self-understanding. More on that later. So I do agree with your thesis that Jesus neither publicly passed himself off as, nor secretly held himself to be, the Messiah in the sense of the theo-political messianic expectations of Israel. This can easily be checked in any concordance: Jesus never applied the titles, Messiah (Christ), Son of David, and Son of God—associated with such expectations, to himself in any saying that can with some probability be traced back to him.[1]

B. The objection which now suggests itself is obvious: the New Testament confesses Jesus as the Son of God, as the Son of David, and above all as the Christ. How are we to understand this, if Jesus never considered himself to be any of these? The foremost title, Christ, became so important early on, probably already during the time of Paul, that it was understood by many as a sort of surname for Jesus. And in the end it is for this reason that we are called "Christians," that is, "Messianists." In any case an indisputable tension exists between the fact that almost from the beginning Christians confessed Jesus as the Christ, that is, as the Messiah, and the fact that Jesus according to his own words did not profess to be the Messiah, or lay claim to the title by behaving as if he were. How can this tension be overcome? Two factors must be taken into account: First there is the Easter faith of the first Christians, which allowed them to see Jesus in a new and deeper light. The Easter experiences meant that God regarded Jesus and his claim favorably and affirmed him. In order to communicate this, the first Christians used expressions common to their own Jewish mode of thought, expressions which Jesus himself did not use. When they said, "Jesus is truly the Messiah," they did not mean that Jesus simply slipped into the role of the Messiah awaited by Israel and so confirmed Israel's expectations. For Jews, the role of the awaited Messiah was primarily political, Israel's liberation from the yoke of the Gentiles. The first Christians who confessed Jesus as the Messiah also knew that this was not what Jesus brought, or intended to bring.

To accentuate what the first Christians did when they confessed, "Jesus is the Messiah," we would have to accentuate, "*Jesus* is the Messiah." And this means that through Jesus, through his works, his words and his death and resurrection, traditional messianic expectations have been fulfilled in a unique manner, transformed and transcended. In Jesus God has spoken in an unexpected, new, and final way, making the expectation of *another* Messiah superfluous for those Jews who believe in Jesus. Indeed, we can probably resolve something even more specific at least about the origin of the title *Christ*. All of the Gospel accounts agree that Jesus was crucified by the Romans. "The inscription of the charge against him read, 'The King of the Jews' " (Mark 15:26). This inscription, which was hung on Jesus' cross, could have been formulated that way only by the Romans, not by the Jews or by Christians.[2] Consequently, Jesus was charged with wanting to be "King of the Jews" and executed by the Romans, for whom this charge was one of treason. To Jewish ears, however, it suggested messianic expectations, for the Messiah was the long-awaited King of Israel. Then, following Easter, Christians appropriated this (false!) indictment against Jesus in a positive sense and confessed that indeed Jesus was the Messiah but not in the political sense which Pilate and perhaps the Jerusalem aristocracy had claimed in their accusation.

Now, having made these two preliminary remarks, the one limiting or qualifying, and the other an attempt more precisely to define the Christian confession of Jesus as the Messiah, I willingly join you in clearing away the next stone from the path to our conversation about Jesus: It is also my opinion that Jesus did not personally consider himself to be the theo-political Messiah awaited by Israel. Nor did Israel—by rejecting Jesus—betray its own faith, as the Gospel of John later suggests. In the Johannine account of Jesus' trial the Jews are portrayed with grandiose perversion as the ones who by rejecting Jesus denied their own faith, their own expectation of the Messiah. "We have no king but Caesar" (John 19:15). Unfortunately, this statement of the Johannine passion narrative is a perfect example of how the image of the Jews—gravely distorted by the post-Easter experience of schism between Christianity and Judaism and by the exclusion of Christians from the synagogue (John 9:22; 12:42; 16:2)—was transformed and removed from reality. The Jews became a symbolic figure representing the world's rejection of Christ. That this was an injustice for the actual Jews is undeniable. In the Gospel of John the actual Jews became a theological symbol. And the theological symbol in turn later became a whipping cane for the actual Jews. Centuries filled with the tragic experiences of your people testify to this.

When I as a Christian theologian say, "Jesus more than likely did not consider himself to be the Messiah in the sense of the Jewish expectation of a theo-political Messiah," I am merely expressing a truism accepted by most Christian theologians. There can hardly be any disagreement about this among Christian New Testament scholars who are concerned with historical honesty. And yet your statement, "These facts . . . are slowly beginning to be circulated even among nontheologians" (p. 46), is perplexing. Here you touch the actual nerve of the problem, which lies not with Christian theologians, but with the laity. It is not merely as a scholar that I am pained when I see how widespread the mistrust of the laity is, despite all of the accepted and well-founded results of historical criticism. It is a profound disgrace for Christian theology that at the end of the 20th century you must still write more than 20 pages to defend an almost self-evident thesis such as your first one. The reasons for this are varied. As a scholar I am aware that the distrust laity have for the abuses and the exaggerated, unproven hypotheses of historical research is often completely justified. But in this case it should be emphasized that, to the extent any of the findings of historical inquiry are certain, this thesis is surely well-founded. It does not undermine or destroy the Christian faith. Christians have never been of the opinion that Jesus was the Messiah as Israel awaited him, that is, in a political sense. Our confession of Jesus as the Christ has never meant *that.* I also know that it is not your intention to destroy anything of our Christian faith with your thesis. This is all the more reason, in my view, that this first thesis be taken seriously not only in the world of professional theology but also among the laity so that the Christian confession of *Jesus* as the Christ no longer becomes a cudgel under which your people suffer. It would be better if we would listen to each other and note that the Jew who says, "Jesus was not the Messiah we were waiting for," does not mean the same thing by the word "Messiah" as the Christian who confesses, "*Jesus* is the Christ" means by the word "Christ."

Very little needs to be said about particular historical problems. Even though I am in total agreement with your overall conclusion, I could not go along with some of your individual arguments, mostly because I do not consider many of the passages you refer to as historical in any real sense; among others, for example, is Jesus' command that the disciples remain silent (p. 35), or the lack of understanding exhibited by the disciples which, according to Mark's account of Peter's confession (Mark 8:27ff.) is not related to Jesus' messiahship but rather to the fact that it is necessary for the Son of man to suffer. I would stress, more strongly than you do, that Jesus' activities are far removed from any direct political action. Naturally, his proclamation of the imminent rule of God, or his summons to love one's enemies and renounce the use of force have considerable indirect political significance. But the goal of Jesus' activity is not truly political—for example, to liberate Israel from the foreign rule of the Romans. This is evidenced in his reply to the question about tribute money: "Render to Caesar the things that are Caesar's, and"—even more importantly, that for which the Pharisees had not called—"to God the things that are God's" (Mark 12:17). It is also evidenced particularly in the passage which could most easily be claimed as a "messianic" action of Jesus, namely, the driving of the merchants and money changers from the temple (Mark 11:15ff.). Time and again this has been presumed to be a "messianic" deed and interpreted, for example, as a forcible occupation of the temple grounds intended to signal the onset of a rebellion against Rome and the temple aristocracy aligned with Rome. This view, however, overlooks the fact that the course of the passion history would have been entirely different if this scene would have been anything more than a prophetic symbol enacted somewhere in a corner of the outer court of the temple. The Roman cohort was regularly stationed in the Antonia fortress, directly adjacent to the temple grounds (Jos. *War* 5.244), and would immediately have intervened in such a disturbance (see Acts 21:31ff.). Moreover, it would remain completely incomprehensible why Jesus on the same evening again withdrew publicly from the temple grounds.

The only question which remains for me is whether Jesus' public appearance may not inadvertently have awakened messianic hopes in the circle of his followers, hopes which in no way reflected his own intentions. John 6:14f. may contain an indication of this. But perhaps the most significant indication is incorporated into the story of Jesus' entry into Jerusalem (Mark 11:lff.), which in my opinion still holds a number of uncertainties. I thoroughly agree with you that the cry of salvation, "Hosanna! Blessed is he who comes in the name of the Lord! Blessed is the kingdom of our father David that is coming! Hosanna in the highest!" (Mark 11:9-10), is in no way messianic (p. 41). Nevertheless, the reference in Mark 11:8, which obviously belongs to the older core of the story, remains conspicuous: "And many spread their garments on the road, and others spread leafy branches which they had cut from the fields." People did not do that for every pilgrim who came from abroad. For me it remains an open question whether Jesus' entrance into Jerusalem may not have awakened messianic hopes among the Galilean followers who were accompanying him, and perhaps even become the occasion for a minor messianic demonstration. We simply do not know. And we know even less about what Jesus may have thought of it, although in the context of the total account, this statement remains relatively insignificant. Such a thesis, however, would help to clarify why Jesus' followers could, after Easter, take over the inscription on the cross which was obviously intended as an indictment of Jesus and make it their confession.

On the whole we are in agreement concerning your first thesis. This does not isolate me among Christian theologians. But I surely also hope we can agree that your first thesis in no way clarifies the mystery of Jesus. If indeed Jesus did not fulfill the messianic role anticipated by Israel, how are we to describe his self-understanding? With this question, however, I am already touching upon the questions you in your summary propose for our future dialog.

Response to Thesis Two

The people of Israel did not reject Jesus.

Your second thesis is clear and simple: Israel did not reject Jesus. In fact many, perhaps even the majority, of the people accepted him. Jesus' trial was essentially a Roman trial that concluded with a Roman verdict. Israel rejected only the deified, heavenly Christ of later Gentile Christendom (p. 83), because he brought Israel into conflict with the basic command to worship *one* God (Deut. 6:4). Rather, it was the Christian sources—primarily John's Gospel, secondly Matthew's, and least of all Luke's—that slandered the Jews and increasingly burdened the entire people of Israel with guilt for Jesus' death in order to exonerate the Romans. So Israel, quite apart from having already been despised and ostracized after the zealot uprisings, now became the scapegoat that had to suffer so that the emerging conflict between Christians and the Roman state could be alleviated.

Regarding the broad strokes, I believe you are correct, even though the course of events itself is not always clear, and we shall have to probe much deeper into many things.

First, regarding Jesus: The list of passages which show that Jesus attracted crowds and was accepted positively by the common folk of Galilee as well as Judea is legion. Most of them are from the evangelists, who had their own reasons for portraying Jesus in this way, as a success among his own people. Sometimes we also hear the opposite: his rejection by the citizens of Nazareth (Mark 6:1ff.), Bethsaida, Chorazin, and even in Capernaum (Matt. 11:20ff.). But I too see no reason why we should mistrust the overall impression of the Gospels, which imply that Jesus found widespread and positive response among his people. This is also in keeping with his proclamation: His message of God's love for everyone, especially for the poor, for women, for the outcast, for sinners and Samaritans, must have opened the hearts of these people to him. His detachment from the laws governing purity, which he often set aside in his healing of the ill, his relativizing of the rules concerning the tithe in favor of the weightier matters of justice, mercy, and faith (Matt. 23:23), and his critical attitude toward the Sadducean rulers of the temple in Jerusalem (see Mark 11:15ff.), must have attracted the good will of those who were discriminated against by these regulations and their application—those who were considered unclean because of their sex or occupation, women and tax collectors, for example; those for whom the tithe meant an almost unbearable burden, that is, the poor; and those who did not directly benefit from the temple and its Sadducean ceremonies, especially the Galileans. In addition, Jesus' proclamation is characterized by great simplicity and clarity. His parables are taken from daily life. In a word, it is a proclamation drawn from the experiences of the people and intended for the people. These reasons alone, it seems to me, make it impossible for anyone to support the thesis that Israel as a whole rejected Jesus.

He was certainly rejected by the Sadducees in Jerusalem, that is, by the top level of the priesthood, who saw their cultic privileges threatened by Jesus' proclamation, and who may also have considered him a dangerous agitator, a disturber of political peace and of the status quo. The case of a Jew being delivered to the Roman authorities by Jews because he announced the destruction of the temple and of Jerusalem is not unique in the first century after Christ.[3]

Jesus was certainly also rejected by many Pharisees. His liberal interpretation of the Sabbath laws and especially his freedom regarding the regulations governing ritual cleanliness must have appeared problematic to the Pharisees, one of whose chief concerns was the ritual purity of the *whole* people of God (Israel), though it is also true that the points of contact between Jesus and the Pharisees are particularly close. I for one do not consider that the numerous scenes in the Gospels which speak of conflict between Jesus and the Pharisees have all been fabricated, even though it can be demonstrated that the Pharisees are increasingly labeled as the *sole* and uncompromising opponents of Jesus in subsequent gospel tradition. Yet given this reality it is all the more conspicuous that the first three Gospels report nothing of the Pharisees participating in the execution of Jesus.[4] This silence which contradicts their normal inclination certainly earns them credence.

You are most likely right in saying that Jesus also had opponents, as did every staunch and uncompromising Jew. But that the people of Israel as a whole rejected him is a falsehood found not even in the Gospel of John. In connection with Jesus' trial, it may well have been an informal gathering of those who opposed Jesus from the circles of the Sadducean priesthood and the Jerusalem aristocracy who agreed to hand Jesus over to the procurator Pilate. But it surely was not a formal session of the whole council, as the Gospel of Mark reports, since the Pharisees are not mentioned as having participated. Moreover, Mark's description mocks every known Jewish code of rules.

The question then remains: What was the origin of this post-Easter schism between those who believed in Jesus and the other Jews, between church and synagogue—this breach which perhaps was unnecessary, and which has brought Israel so much suffering? To formulate it even more pointedly: how did it happen that the loyalty to the faith which Jesus himself professed was charged against the Jews as unbelief from the Christian side? What was the origin of the obvious attempt increasingly to depict everything in either-or categories? What is the origin of the collective and simplistic sevenfold "woes" on the scribes and Pharisees, which have nothing whatever favorable to report (Matthew 23)? What is the origin of the harsh statement in Matthew's Gospel which suddenly views the masses, usually open to Jesus, as Jesus' enemies along with their leaders, and allows them to curse themselves: "And all the people answered, 'His blood be on us and on our children!' " (Matt. 27:25)? This statement, found only in Matthew, was certainly not uttered during Jesus' passion. It must have been introduced by Matthew who saw it as being fulfilled with the destruction of Jerusalem (A.D. 70). But he could scarcely have known that this comment would be partly responsible for the shedding of the blood of the children of Israel on innumerable subsequent occasions. How did the book of Revelation come to speak of "a synagogue of Satan" (Rev. 2:9; 3:9), and the Gospel of John of the devil as the father of the

Jews (John 8:44)? And finally, to break off this shameful enumeration, how did the New Testament itself, our Christian source of faith, become a source—in fact, a highly effective historical source—of anti-Semitism? How could *Christian* anti-Semitism ever have come about?

This is the question that torments me most. It begins where your second thesis ends, but you clearly suggested it in your text. And even if you as a Jew had remained silent, I as a Christian would have had to deal with it. It is a question that cuts to the quick because, to a greater or lesser extent, it touches *all* writings of the New Testament. We can't help but be moved by it because it is aimed directly at the New Testament which is and remains the great charter of our Christian faith. This makes it difficult for us to regard all of the excesses of Christian anti-Semitism, which we must now look back on, merely as regrettable mistakes, and simply return to the order of the day. The thorn penetrates much deeper. The theological fathers to whom you refer—Chrysostom, the "golden-mouthed" orator, the later Luther, and many from our own day whom you quote—also have *their* fathers; and they are none other than several of the New Testament authors. How did this come about?

In my opinion, the critical reappraisal of this material must be one of the most essential tasks of a future conversation between Christians and Jews, if our meeting is ever to lead to an authentic mastery of the past and not merely to a superficial retouching of, or a rash disassociation from, fragmentary New Testament expressions. It is my opinion that our first job must be to *understand* these difficult, often cruel New Testament expressions. To understand does not mean to sanction or excuse; but without understanding, no learning or sound critique is possible.

I do not wish to anticipate the coming conversation here. Instead I shall merely state in thesis fashion several points and questions that seem to me to be pertinent. You have yourself indicated the importance of political apologetic (the arrangement between Christians and Romans at the expense of the Jews, pp. 77f.), and the transformation of Jesus into a non-Jewish divine figure, which in turn transformed Christianity from a Jewish sect into a Hellenistic religion of salvation (p. 83). Without a doubt these two factors do play an important role. I would, however, like to expand the palette with a few additional considerations.

It is apparent that the front between Christians and Jews in the New Testament is often notably more abrupt when an author is in fact particularly close to Judaism. This is clearly the case for the most Jewish of New Testament books, the Revelation of John, which more than likely was finally edited by Palestinian immigrants on the basis of Palestinian traditions in Asia Minor during the reign of Domitian (81-97). Among the evangelists, the things we find in Matthew are especially informative: among his principal concerns are the keeping of the law (5:17-19) and the preservation of the Old Testament for the church, represented programmatically by his use of so-called formula quotations (for example, Matt. 1:22f.; 2:5f., 15, 23; etc.). Precisely this most Jewish of the evangelists has so marked himself by his exceptionally blunt attack on Israel that one exegete could say that Matthew has "cut up . . . the table cloth" held in common with Israel,[5] and is now fighting with Israel for the inheritance. In reality the "table cloth" had already been cut during the period before Matthew. Tradition speaks of various persecutions (Matt. 5:12f.; 22:5; 23:29ff.) and of an unsuccessful mission to Israel (23:37ff.). Matthew looks back to the painful litigation that led to the divorce of his congregation from the synagogue; he refers to "your," that is, to "their" synagogues (4:23; 9:35; 23:34; etc.). Nevertheless it is still of vital importance to him, as a Jewish Christian, that the God of Jesus is the God of the Old Testament, and that the mission of Jesus is planned and accomplished by this God. Thus fraternal strife erupted at the very point where the relationship between hostile siblings was particularly close and particularly intense. Something similar can also be said about the Gospel of John. That is, the conflict often flared up with exceptional intensity, and the rift became woefully deep, precisely where Christianity had remained particularly close to its Jewish foundations, rather than where as a Hellenistic religion of salvation it had departed from its Jewish roots (where it had inherited Jewish traditions but had forgotten the Jews!). Perhaps it can also be said that the emergence of Christian anti-Semitism is a problem characteristically associated with the breaking of a close mother-child relationship or, expressed differently, a unique problem of apostasy.

That brings me to the next question. Why didn't Israel remain the target group to whom Jesus' followers addressed their proclamation, as Jesus had? Or, conversely, why didn't Jesus' followers remain in the bosom of Israel? What brought about the break between the synagogues and the Christian communities? The latter did not really want to become a sectarian group, to say nothing of being an autonomous religion; they carried out their severance from Israel involuntarily. Here, too, careful attention must be paid to nuances: Jewish experience shows that confessing a particular person to be the Messiah was by no means sufficient reason for expulsion from the synagogue.[6] Even the confession of an individual's resurrection did not of necessity have that consequence.[7] The arguments surrounding the Stephen circle in Jerusalem and the proceedings at the apostolic council indicate that the question of keeping the Torah, which had become particularly acute because of the Gentile mission, contributed substantially to the conflict.[8] At this point the question arises of the extent to which relativizing and reinterpretation of the law from the perspective of the kingdom of God may already have been the seed that led to the conflict of Stephen's followers with Judaism. Both factors—the Torah and the confession of Jesus as the Christ or as the Son of man—may well have played a role in the debate. Over and above this we must also ask to what extent external, nontheological factors were of significance. Here I am thinking of the animosity of the leading circles of Jerusalem who opposed Jesus during his lifetime and more than likely remained opponents of his followers after Easter. Certainly the tense situation throughout Palestine in the wake of the zealot uprisings, which increasingly pressed for purification, separation, and exclusion rather than for openness and inclusivity, must be taken into account. And of course, the fact that early Christianity soon had its greatest successes in the area of Gentile missions alienated the synagogues of the so-called God-fearers, and as a consequence *had to be* treated with greater severity than any of the other schismatic Jewish sects, cannot be overlooked. In a word, we know that among other factors, the break between the synagogue and the developing church in the first century, with all of its traumatic consequences, became a basic presupposition for Christian anti-Semitism. But whether this was the inevitable result of things or whether, viewed historically, it was merely a coincidental fact, is still an open question. Its various ramifications must be discussed fully in mutual conversation.

Finally, allow me to mention one further point which I feel

contributed substantially to the fact that the Christian image of the Jews was increasingly removed from reality and could therefore be determined primarily by theological or, rather, ideological factors: The disappearance of a living Jewish encounter as a result of the break between church and synagogue. Early Christian theology was shaped by its debate with Judaism. For Christian missionaries, the experience of unbelief in Christ was as important as that of (moral) sin, and they used Israel as a prime example of the former. Theological reflection in turn soon led to such pointed Pauline and Johannine statements as: "The Counselor . . . will convince the world of sin . . . because they do not believe in me" (John 16:7-9) or, "Whatever does not proceed from faith is sin" (Rom. 14:23). Paul is thinking in conventional Jewish ways when he speaks of the epitome of sin as being the rejection of God, the exchanging of creation for the Creator, or the reliance upon one's own righteousness at the expense of God's grace.[9] Nevertheless, he comes dangerously close to a *moral* condemnation of unbelief as "sin" in the usual sense of the word. That is to say, he encourages such a misunderstanding by using the many-faceted and iridescent word "sin." When a living Jewish encounter—in which response, instruction, and correction could take place—disappeared, leaving only the tradition of early Christendom, the Christian image of the Jews almost inevitably oriented itself according to the *theological* judgment at which the New Testament authors had arrived through their living debate with Judaism. In other words, a theological opinion that had emerged out of a living debate and bore all of the imbalances and biases characteristic of such a formative situation later replaced the debate with living Jews which was no longer possible because the Jews were now "outsiders." On both sides possibilities for dialog no longer existed. This eventually led to the abstract theological concepts, "synagogue" and "Judaism," which we simply borrowed from the New Testament, without verifying them in a living encounter. And that is why even theologians who certainly cannot be accused of anti-Semitism still speak of the synagogue in an abstract sense as representing "unbelief," without ever realizing that such symbolism condemns actual persons and triggers reactions which they themselves would dread.[10]

Jews and Christians called upon the same God and appealed to the same Old Testament, but in different ways. This led to conflict and fraternal strife, which in turn resulted in alienation, detachment, and unrelatedness. Finally, unrelatedness allowed the theological judgments that had arisen out of a living encounter to become fixed as abstract systems that were then actually used to strike at real people. All of this can be overcome only by engaging in dialog. We Christians cannot afford to shut ourselves off from our Jewish brothers and sisters, especially if we wish to come to a new, yet critical and just understanding of the pointedly anti-Jewish statements of the New Testament that stand between us.

Response to Thesis Three

Jesus never repudiated his people.

I also agree with this thesis. Strictly speaking, none of the Gospels champions the counterthesis, not even Matthew, whose interpretation of the parable of the vineyard you examine in detail. Matthew does affirm the second of the theses you repudiate (that Israel has rejected Jesus), but not the third. His thesis is set forth in the parable of the vineyard (21:33-44), in the parable of the marriage feast (22:1-14), and, above all, in the curse which the people call down upon themselves (27:25): The Jews have rejected Jesus and so have lost their place as God's chosen people. God will therefore give the kingdom promised them to another people, the church, provided that it produces the fruits of the kingdom (21:43). Matthew most likely saw in the destruction of Jerusalem in the year 70 the fulfillment of the curse which the people called down upon themselves before Pilate. Whether he thought there was still a possibility for Israel to be saved is uncertain. But Jesus himself, even according to Matthew, never rejected Israel; he remained Israel's Messiah who was sent to the lost sheep of his own people (Matt. 10:5f.; 15:24).

Luke argues even more clearly, depicting both Jesus and the apostles after his death as having great success throughout Israel and in its very center, in Jerusalem and in the temple. He can even speak of the Pentecost community as still "having favor with all the people" (Acts 2:47). According to Luke the pages of history turn slowly. The dispersion of the early church after the martyrdom of Stephen signals the first note of a new era in the post-Easter story, an era in which the rejection of the gospel by Israel—but never by all Israel—becomes ever more apparent. In view of the blunt words the Johannine Jesus speaks against the Jews we might assume that, at least in the eyes of this evangelist, Jesus repudiated his people. But even according to John the decisive factor is that the majority of the people rejected Jesus and by doing so became untrue to their own faith, to the Old Testament promises, and to their own messianic expectations. You yourself have underscored how emphatically even John can speak about Jews who have come to faith (pp. 72f.). This in itself shows that we most likely do no justice even to John when we say that Jesus rejected Israel.

Thus, regarding this thesis, there is consensus even among the evangelists. If at this point in my reply I don't simply lay my pen aside, but continue to write, it is because I feel we ought to reflect a bit on *how* Jesus knew that he had been sent to his people and what was particularly important to him. Let me note a few items I consider important to the continuation of our dialog about Jesus:

A. First something negative. It is striking to me how little concern Jesus seems to have had for the "national" question.

And yet this question is not unwarranted or irrelevant simply because it is political—quite the contrary. For Israel the so-called national question was actually a theological question. The fact that Israel was subject to Roman authority and that taxes had to be paid to a pagan nation for the very soil of the holy land was a direct provocation of God. What of God's faithfulness to his Word? What of God's promises? Is it not remarkable how little Jesus seems to think about this point? He doesn't answer the related question about taxes directly (Mark 12:13-17). Nor is there ever a political sharpening of the petition, "Your kingdom come."[11] Why?

B. Yet another negative. Jesus seems not at all interested in the laws of the people of Israel. The Ten Commandments interest him, as the first two antitheses of the Sermon on the Mount indicate (Matt. 5:21f., 27f.), not from the perspective of a lawgiver but because of their ethical values. He demands the love of one's enemies, the renunciation of force, and even calls for his followers to relinquish their possessions, apparently without ever giving a thought to the consequences such demands would have on Israel's rights. He forbids divorce and the remarriage of those who have been divorced on the basis of a radical understanding of God's will for creation—again without ever giving a thought to the question whether the prohibition of divorce can be legally enforced or, indeed, without even considering the harmful social consequences that the prohibition of the remarriage of divorced women might possibly have. He says, "Judge not, that you be not judged" (Matt. 7:1). Viewed against a Jewish backdrop this is a rather amazing statement which, to all appearances, completely disregards the fact that for Israel, Torah is a special gift of God and the central expression of God's election. It also ignores the fact that, insofar as it was possible, Israel—with good reason, even in times of foreign rule—always struggled to judge according to its Torah, that is, in accordance with God's Law. Joseph Klausner, in my opinion, justifiably expresses displeasure with Jesus' polemic against the ceremonial law, charging that he overlooked the fact that it was precisely the ceremonial law that distinguished Israel from all other peoples and constituted its peculiarity.[12] Jesus seems not to be concerned about that. Correspondingly, he never speaks of God's covenant with his people, apart from the uncertain word spoken in connection with the passing of the cup at the Last Supper (Mark 14:24). Why?

C. For me the key to an answer to both of these questions lies in the fact that Jesus' primary attention was directed to Israel's future in God's kingdom and not so much to Israel's present character before the onset of God's kingdom. The inner circle of the Twelve which Jesus selected from among his closest followers, it seems to me, is an expression of this orientation. We can interpret it in no other way than as an eschatological representation of the twelve tribes. The only truly helpful passage (Matt. 19:28) also points in this direction. The circle of the Twelve is the anticipation of the eschatological fullness of God's people which will become a visible reality in God's kingdom. As is well known, the circle of the Twelve contains something of a utopian element, which becomes apparent the moment one thinks of the people of Israel during Jesus' time. Even according to their own understanding, only the two tribes that had remained in the land were included, and it was assumed that the remaining tribes, which presumably lived in exile somewhere in the distant north or east, would, at the end of history, again be led back to the land of Israel. With the circle of the Twelve Jesus certainly revealed his devotion for Israel and his claim upon the whole of Israel. But at the same time he showed that at this point in his mission, he also saw the dawning of eschatological fulfillment.

D. A further point is connected with Jesus' eschatological perspective. God's love breaks through the boundaries that had been established for Israel, generally by the Torah itself. Most often Jesus showed compassion for outsiders and marginal people. He directed his attention primarily to those who, in the opinion of some, could no longer be counted among true Israel: to tax collectors, a notoriously despised occupation suspected of being unclean; to outcasts and possessed; and to women, among whom prostitutes are given particular prominence in the tradition. A fine example is the story of the good Samaritan, which demonstrates that precisely the despised Samaritan, about whose inclusion among God's people there were various opinions, came closer to fulfilling the will of God by caring for the man who had fallen among robbers than did the respected priest or Levite who passed by on the other side. "Which of these three, do you think, proved neighbor to the man who fell among the robbers?" (Luke 10:36). Formulated in a situation where the problem of the relationship of Jews to Samaritans was no longer relevant, Luke's concluding question is adapted to provide what we today also recognize as a good example of neighborly love (see Luke 10:37). Other Jewish groups, for example, the Essenes, who lived in camps or cloister-like settlements such as Qumran, drew the circle around Israel tightly: only those who kept the Law in its most rigorous sense could count themselves as the holy remnant of Israel. Jesus, on the contrary, opened the boundaries. God's love was for all, particularly for marginal peoples, the outcasts, and the despised.

E. Given this tendency toward viewing Israel as being open on the basis of God's limitless love, Jesus' attitude toward the Gentiles must also be reexamined. Two stories speak of Jesus' encounter with Gentiles: the story of the centurion in Capernaum (Matt. 8:5ff.) and the story of the Syrophoenician woman (Mark 7:24ff.). Neither story allows us to speak of any basic openness toward Gentiles on Jesus' part; rather, each in its own way depicts Jesus as preserving the preeminence of Israel. If the ancient saying, "Many will come from east and west and sit at table with Abraham, Isaac, and Jacob in the kingdom of heaven, while the sons of the kingdom will be thrown into the outer darkness" (Matt. 8:11f.), could be traced to Jesus, we would have evidence to show that Jesus counted on an influx of the Gentiles at the time of the kingdom's future fulfillment rather than in the present. Nevertheless, in determining whether the openness to a Gentile mission (which the church actually undertook after Easter) is truly legitimate from the perspective of Jesus' own proclamation, we must take into account the limitless love of God which lies at the core of Jesus' eschatological proclamation.

F. The eschatological perspective of Jesus' proclamation also hangs together with the idea of judgment in a similar way. Judgment is not suspended for Israel. Rather, in the tradition of the prophets, Jesus sees the threat of judgment directed especially to Israel. The warning of the judgment which will break in as suddenly as it did in the days of Noah and Lot (Luke 17:26-30) is meant for the same Israel to whom Jesus promises God's limitless and unconditional love. There will be no salvation *only* because one belongs to Israel. Such thinking does not distinguish Jesus from the Jewish convictions of his time, especially not from the prophetic tradition with which he had a close relationship. More than likely he also stands in the prophetic-apocalyptic tradition with his word of judgment about the future destruction of the temple (for example, Mark 14:58). This word occurs so often in the tradition that I must disagree with you (pp. 104f.) and, despite the protests of the evangelists themselves, ask whether it could not after all be traced back to Jesus in some form or other.[13] In the word of judgment referred to above (Matt. 8:11f.) Jesus pointedly directs his thoughts entirely against Israel, comparable only to the prophecy of Amos. Certainly he does not intend to say that Israel would forfeit salvation. Rather, this threat is formulated sharply, for rhetorical purposes: It could happen that. . . . With the message that the kingdom of God is at hand, even Israel is challenged to make a decision. Jesus does not leave the framework of prophetic thought until he concentrates this decision totally on his own person, his work, and his message.

> Every one who acknowledges me before men, the Son of man also will acknowledge before the angels of God; but he who denies me before men will be denied before the angels of God (Luke 12:8-9).

No prophet ever dared to speak of himself that way. No one within Judaism, with the possible exception of the Qumran teacher of righteousness,[14] spoke of himself that way. The decisive measure in God's final judgment was never an individual and his message; it was always the Torah.

Jesus knew that he had indeed been sent to his people. But he was not interested primarily in historical Israel, constituted through the Sinai covenant and God's election. Rather his mind was set on eschatological reality, on the fact that with the advent of his kingdom God would, in his limitless love, call together his people out of *all* Israel, including even and especially its most despised members. God, who had initiated the advent of his kingdom and called Jesus to be a witness to its coming, did not suspend his love for Israel with Jesus' coming; he surpassed it, dispensed with its limitations, and broadened as well as deepened it. Jesus in his mission did not simply confirm the election of Israel; he established it anew.

Having said this, we again come face to face with the question of Jesus' self-understanding. It appears to have been unique, even though Jesus did not consider himself the Messiah; and so this continues to remain a decisive theme for a future Jewish-Christian dialog.

However, before I speak of that I would like to emphasize again that in view of the proclamation of Jesus I am completely in agreement with the conclusions of your third chapter (pp. 109-110):

- if the boundless love of God for sinners was at the heart of Jesus' proclamation;
- if the community interpreted his death as a ransom for *many* (Mark 10:45; 14:24);
- if it confessed that God "did not spare his own Son but gave him up for us *all*" (Rom. 8:32);
- if Paul interpreted the gospel as justification alone by God's grace, for Jews as *Jews* and for Gentiles as Gentiles—

then in fact no church dare declare God's love an ecclesiastical monopoly and limit it to the narrow confines of its own walls. It must rather say with Paul: If God so loves us Gentiles, how much more will he remain faithful to his own people, for whom election and the promises were intended and remain in effect!

Concerning the dialog for tomorrow

The purpose of our little book was to remove stones from the way so that the dialog for tomorrow could begin. Let me in conclusion therefore also look to tomorrow and reflect a bit about this future dialog.

I do not now wish to speak of the many other important themes that might be dealt with in such a dialog, but only of the theme which was the subject of this book—Jesus. What open, burning questions remain here that should be explored mutually?

The question that interests me most is a question which you did not address directly, but which I nevertheless detect behind the view of Jesus that is sketched out in your book. You, more than likely, never raised it yourself because of your concern for the impartiality of the dialog, leaving it for your Christian partner to pose. It can be formulated as follows:

If Jesus was a true Jew who confessed the God of Israel and believed in him, who perceived himself as being sent to the people of Israel and to no one else, a Jew who was a human being, who would have felt decidedly strange in the divine heights to which Greek theology later elevated him, a Jew who, according to you, kept the Torah (p. 92), then the primary question is not whether Jews can consider Jesus their brother, the way many in Jesus' own lifetime did and many today still do. Rather, the question is whether the Christian churches can rightfully appeal to Jesus, not merely as *one* of their brothers, but as *the* beginning, the foundation, and the goal of their faith. The primary question is certainly not whether Jesus belongs to Judaism, but rather, whether we as Christians have not so transformed Jesus that we can reclaim him only if we transform ourselves.

Is there a trajectory that can proceed from Jesus to Christendom? Is there a trajectory from the man Jesus to the second person of the Trinity? Is there a path from the mission of Jesus to Israel to the mission to the Gentiles? Is there a line from Jesus' expectation of the kingdom of God to faith in Jesus' saving death, his death on our behalf for the forgiveness of sins, and the mystery of the resurrection? Is there a line from Jesus' faithfulness to the Torah to the Pauline statement that Jesus is the end of the Law (Rom. 10:4)?

Put in still another way: Is the identity between Christian faith and Jewish faith so great that—to use a catchword of Shalom ben Chorin in a different context—Jesus can be "fraternally shared in fraternity"? Or is the difference between Jews and Christians, as well as between contemporary Christendom and its origins, finally so great that it would be better for us not to gloss it over with a Jesus we hold in common? Has what you refer to (p. 114) as the "irreducible residue" of the earthly Jesus, which firmly resists all mythification, deification, and theologizing, really remained decisive for the Christian faith, or is in fact the myth—the Son of God, the bringer of salvation, the Christ of faith—of greater importance? Is the spread of Christian monotheism in the western world, which you gratefully acknowledge as God's way, not a *de facto* de-Judaizing of the God of Israel? The primary question for us Christians must be: Can *we* call upon Jesus as *the* (not merely one!) ground of our faith at all?

This question contains much explosive material. In one of our conversations we once stated that because of what has happened in our history it was high time that a Jewish-Christian dialog be conducted with Judaism taking the offensive and Christianity the defensive. Actually it is really a pity that you did not radically pursue the offensive. I find your approach a sort of offensively executed defense, but not a real offensive (even though at several points the course such an offensive would take becomes apparent). This being the case, I would like to anticipate something of the coming dialog, or at least mark the points at which it must take place and indicate several basic factors that I have incorporated into my position and that characterize it.

I am convinced of three things: *First, Christianity must appeal to Jesus*—not merely to the "that" of his coming, not merely to his name, which can be filled with almost any content desired—*if it wants to endure* without allowing itself to be transformed willy-nilly by anyone and by every historical epoch. It *must* appeal to Jesus, as long as it continues to affirm that God acted historically in Jesus and not merely in our momentary faith experiences and ideas.

Second, I am convinced that appealing to Jesus cannot be painless and without consequences for us in the present; rather, it demands that our churches modify their theology and practice.

Third, I believe that it is possible for the church to appeal to Jesus; that is, there is a trajectory from Jesus to Christ, from the kingdom of God Jesus anticipated to faith in his saving death and resurrection, from his own understanding of Torah to the Christ of Paul who is the end of the Law (Rom. 10:4). I am convinced—to take up a point that must perhaps continue to remain controversial between us—that Jesus according to his own self-understanding cannot simply be classified as *one* among many pious Jews, who may have expressed and enriched the faith of Israel in an exemplary fashion. Rather, it is my conviction that a response to Jesus involves taking a position on his claim of having been given a *unique role* and a *unique commission* by God. That is to say, a response to Jesus that affirms him and his message, yet considers him merely *one* of many in the great series of fathers of the Jewish faith, does not, in my opinion, do him justice; moreover, it contains a negation at least of his claim of wanting to be more, decisively more, than just another prophet or teacher of Torah among many. This does not exclude the possibility that the Christian responses to Jesus, i.e., the post-Easter confession of his uniqueness and indispensability, have at many points forgotten or supplanted the concrete form of his activity and have spiritualized, theorized, and idolized him, thereby also making him harmless. However, the basic *dimension* of the post-Easter response to Jesus appears to me to correspond with his own claim.

Perhaps you may now think: "These crafty Christians! First they agree completely, even admitting that Jesus was not the Messiah; then they smuggle his messiahship back in through the back door, larger, even more unassailable—because it is more indefinable—than it was before!" No! That is not my intention. I do not mean that Jesus considered himself to be the Messiah in the theo-political sense anticipated by Israel, but something completely different. I also do not mean that the rejection of Jesus' claim in any way imposed guilt on, or contradicted the basic confession of, the Jewish faith. To the contrary, I agree with you now as I did before, that a Jewish affirmation, at least of *certain* Christian responses to Jesus, would have led to a contradiction of the basic confession of Israel's faith. Israel *can* not follow the way of freedom from Torah, because God *gave* (not imposed as a burden!) *them* (not the Gentiles!) the way of Torah. Moreover, even with Christ, the way of Israel must, because of the Law, still remain a different way than that of the Gentiles, if God is not to be accused of not keeping his word. As I see it, even Paul would have said this. Especially from the perspective of Christian theology, so it seems to me, there must be a *particular* way for Israel to follow. Beyond this it is also my opinion that Israel's rejection of certain Christian responses to Jesus can truly raise fundamental questions for us Christians, perhaps because our responses to Jesus actually contradict his own self-understanding. But more about that later.

At the moment it is more important for me to mention a few more thoughts and questions related to the third point I stated above. I believe that a negative response to the question whether Jesus considered himself to be the Messiah in the theo-political sense anticipated by Israel does not yet provide an answer to the question concerning his distinctiveness, indeed, the uniqueness of his self-understanding. In this respect I find the following passages significant: "If it is by the finger of God that I cast out demons, then the kingdom of God has come upon you" (Luke 11:20). "I saw Satan fall like lightning from heaven" (Luke 10:18). "When a strong man, fully armed, guards his own palace, his goods are in peace; but when one stronger than he assails him and overcomes him, he takes away his armor in which he trusted, and divides his spoil" (Luke 11:21-22). It is never *said* in so many words, but it is implied that Jesus sees the awaited kingdom already dawning in his own works, not directly and visibly, but in secret, like a tiny grain of mustard seed in contrast to the great mustard tree (Matt. 13:31-32). Jesus obviously perceives that he has a special function in the dawning of God's promised consummation. "Can the wedding guests fast while the bridegroom is with them?" (Mark 2:19). Whether and how he determines what his role will be remains an open question. In this connection we should at our earliest opportunity speak about the question of the Son of man, a question about which I myself am still uncertain. If it were true that Jesus saw his own work connected in some mysterious and personal way with that of the coming Son of man—which I consider possible—then we would also have a direct linguistic indication of his self-understanding from his own lips. Such an understanding would in no way correspond to the eschatological expectations of Israel, though it could hardly be conceivable without them.

If this were the case it would also be clear that Jesus had established God's will in a new way. The radical summons to love one's enemies corresponds to the love of God which is imparted to humans, beginning with sinners and outcasts, at the advent of his kingdom. In my opinion God's will is established anew in this coming of the kingdom. The Torah as the previous principal expression of God's will recedes rather far into the background. "Every one who acknowledges me before men, the Son of man will acknowledge before the angels of God" (Luke 12:8), declares Jesus, and so makes himself, his coming and his claim, the decisive measure in the final judgment, without even mentioning the Torah. But note that

I do not mean that Jesus sees his interpretation of God's will primarily in opposition to the Torah (though he sets new accents, and at least comes close to doing so regarding the laws regulating purity, which he himself often sets aside for the sake of the ill and the outcast!). Rather, Jesus' primary concern is a deeper and more radical comprehension of the will of God than had previously been made known in the Torah, the will of God seen from the new perspective of the authority and power of the kingdom of God which surpasses everything previous to it and which he proclaims and personifies. That is why he can say, "You have heard that it was said to the men of old [that is, that God spoke to your fathers at Sinai] . . . , but I say to you" (Matt. 5:21f.). With these words Jesus contrasts his interpretation of God's will with that of the Old Testament itself, not just with the interpretation of another rabbinic colleague. Everything that follows, however, does not stand in direct opposition to the content of the Old Testament, but denotes its affirmation and deepening from the vantage point of a new authority.

And finally, we ought carefully to examine whether Jesus himself did not intend his own death to have a very special function and meaning in relationship to the advent of God's kingdom. What is the meaning of that mysterious, ancient word, "I came to cast fire [the fire of the last judgment] upon earth; and would that it were already kindled! I have a submerging to undergo and how I am constrained until it is accomplished!" (Luke 12:49f.; author's trans.)? How is this related to the fact that Jesus obviously did not see his impending death as conflicting with his hope in the approaching kingdom of God: "Truly, I say to you, I shall not drink again of the fruit of the vine until that day when I drink it new in the kingdom of God" (Mark 14:25)? This is the most difficult and uncertain point of all. I do not think it can be demonstrated that Jesus himself spoke of his death as an atonement "for many" (Mark 14:24). But I do think we can establish that Jesus understood his death as a constituent part of his mission and considered it as something irreplaceable, particularly in connection with the advent of God's kingdom.

These are merely suggested questions, not theses or proofs. They make up the list of themes I hope can be pursued in a future conversation about Jesus. As I see it, in spite of everything, they suggest trajectories that lead from Jesus to the Christian faith, lines that lead from Jesus to the Christian confession of the special meaning of his death (though here I still have many questions!), from Jesus' understanding of the Law to Paul's thesis that Jesus is the end of the Law, and from Jesus' message of the radical, limitless love of God for sinners and outcasts, which he himself personified for the outcasts and the destitute among his own people, Israel, on to the post-Easter proclamation of the love of God even to the Gentiles. Though these trajectories may have been deepened and in some cases even severed by Easter, it still seems to me that there is a clear and generally continuous line from Jesus to the Christian confession of his uniqueness and irreplaceability. These are not simply Christian postulates without which I could neither live nor believe; rather, they are theses and questions that have arisen out of my study of Jesus, about which I would like to speak with you. Postulates of a dogmatic nature, e.g., that Jesus *must* have been exceptional or else Christians would not be able to relate exclusively to him and his interpretation of God, are not acceptable to me. If I begin with the assumption that the basis of my faith is a particular activity of God *in history,* then I must also be willing to accept the fact that under the circumstances this history may have looked different from what I imagine, and so I must ask myself whether my faith may not have to be corrected on the basis of a study of this history. I say this to make it clear that in any future conversation about Jesus I am willing to abandon dogmatic premises and Christian conjectures about him.

Above all, however, in view of the second point I previously mentioned, I must again state clearly that for me the thesis that there is a definite trajectory leading from Jesus to the Christian confession of his uniqueness does not mean that each and every Christian confession of Jesus' uniqueness is legitimate. Here it is necessary to make distinctions, and on the basis of Jesus himself. A confession of Jesus' uniqueness that is not actually *lived out* in the sense of Jesus' command to love others as one loves oneself obviously ignores Jesus. It is from this perspective that our questions ought to be directed, not only to Christian history in general, but to the New Testament itself, for example, to the truly oppressive and unjust speech on the Pharisees in Matthew 23. Similarly, the confession of Jesus' divinity may have been unavoidable and quite pertinent for the Greeks and for Europeans of the previous century, whose thought processes had been shaped by Platonic metaphysics, even though it inevitably strained the possibility of a conversation with Israel. However, this confession has always been problematic insofar as it has threatened to swallow the humanity of Jesus as well as the historical reality of his mission; theologically this is the case in its monophysite form, but for me this is also largely true of its Chalcedonian, non-Antiochene form. In my opinion it is impossible for us to go on thinking as the Greeks once did, even though we have learned, and still can learn, much from them.

Perhaps the most important point you touched on, it seems to me, is your question concerning the realization of the promises (pp. 51-53). It is true that Christian thought exhibits a peculiar tendency to spiritualize these promises, that is, to shift God's action from the arena of history to the sphere of inwardness. Unquestionably, the embarrassment of facing a Jewish God in whose active historical involvement we Christians, all the way from the Corinthian enthusiasts to Rudolf Bultmann, have found it difficult to believe plays an important role. As I see it, one of the most important tasks Israel has in Jewish-Christian dialog is to make it as awkward as possible for Christian churches and theologians to evade historical reality by withdrawing into spirituality. More than likely, we Christians have inherited this tendency toward evasiveness primarily through our faith in Jesus' resurrection, which in a sense not only supported but often replaced our anticipation for the kingdom of God which is yet to come. From this perspective, faith in the resurrection of Jesus has an ambivalent aspect, and this not only as I see it, in its adaptation to the beliefs of the Hellenistic mystery religions. I believe, hope, and expect that in this case "unbelieving" Israel may well have the special task in the history of salvation of calling the "believing" church to its true purpose (e.g., regarding this very matter).

But in saying this I am already becoming involved in the plans of God and my theological conscience bids me stop. Besides, I believe it is time to close; I have tried your patience and the patience of our readers long enough. I hope that from what I have said you will recognize how much I look forward to the dialog of "tomorrow." May "tomorrow" come quickly.

With cordial greetings,
Ulrich Luz

Notes

Part One
A Jewish Perspective by Pinchas Lapide

Introduction

1. Hans Küng, in *Concilium* (1974), no. 10, 543.
2. K. Rahner, "Dein verkannter Bruder," in *Lebendige Kirche* (1961): 4,2.
3. H. Gollwitzer, *Der Ungekündigte Bund* (Stuttgart, 1962), p. 48.
4. Migne, *P.L.*, 178, p. 1609.
5. J. Moltmann, "Der Gott der Hoffnung," in *Gott Heute,* ed. N. Kutschki (Munich, 1967), p. 121.
6. *Israel und die Kirche* (Zurich, 1961), pp. 42f.
7. M. Stöhr, *Antijudaismus im Neuen Testament?* (Munich, 1967), p. 196.
8. *Church Dogmatics* (Edinburgh: T. and T. Clark, 1936-1969), vol. 4.3, p. 878.
9. *Sicut Judaeis non (P.L.,* 214, p. 864).
10. K. Thieme, *Judenfeindschaft* (Frankfurt, 1963), p. 48.
11. J. Maier, "Jesus von Nazareth und sein Verhältnis zum Judentum," in *Jesu Judesein als Zugang zum Judentum,* ed. W. P. Eckert and H. H. Henrix (Handreichung für Religionsunterricht und Erwachsenenbildung; Aachen, 1976), p. 73.

12. The following quotations are from Charlotte Klein, *Anti-Judaism in Christian Theology* (Philadelphia: Fortress, 1978).

Thesis One: Jesus did not declare himself to his people as Messiah

1. R. Bultmann, *Theology of the New Testament* (New York: Scribners, 1951) 1:28.
2. Rabbi, who healed two deaf persons in b.Hag. 3a; Hanina ben Dosa healed through prayer: b.Ber. 34b.
3. Hanina ben Dosa drove out a demon: b.Pes. 112b-113a.
4. R. Gamaliel stilled the storm-tossed waves of the sea through prayer: b.B.Mes. 59b.
5. Hanina's wife, whose oven was filled with bread and whose bowl was filled with dough: b.Taan. 24b-25a.
6. Rabbi (Mekilta Wajehi, Besh. I), like one of his students (Lev.R. 10), could raise the dead.
7. R. Akiba publicly pronounced Bar Kochba as "King Messiah" (b.Taan. 68d).
8. P. Volz, *Die Eschatologie der jüdischen Gemeinde* (Tübingen, 1934), p. 228.
9. H. L. Strack and P. Billerbeck, *Kommentar zum Neuen Testament aus Talmud und Midrasch,* 6 vols. (Munich, 1922-1961), 2:282.
10. Bultmann, *Theology,* 1:31.
11. B.Sukk. 52a, directly from R. Dosa.
12. M. Hengel, *Die Zeloten* (Leiden, 1970), pp. 304f.; also Strack-Billerbeck, 2:292ff., and M. Johnson, *The Purpose of the Biblical Genealogies* (Cambridge: Cambridge University Press, 1969), pp. 129-130.
13. C. Thoma, *Kirche aus Juden und Heiden* (Vienna, 1970), p. 45; see also *A Christian Theology of Judaism* (New York: Paulist, 1980), pp. 59-63.
14. The Sicarii were a fanatic sect within Judaism which even after the removal of the Zealots by the Romans continued the rebellion against Rome.
15. See, for example, Matt. 4:23; 9:35; 13:54; Mark 1:21,39; Luke 4:16ff.; John 6:59; 18:2.
16. Aug., *Serm.* 76.
17. Bultmann, *Theology,* 1:26.
18. E. Schweizer, *Jesus* (Richmond: John Knox, 1971), p. 15.
19. Oscar Cullmann, *Jesus and the Revolutionaries* (New York: Harper and Row, 1970), pp. 40 and 69, n. 15.
20. The quotation is a conflation of Ps. 2:7; Isa. 42:1; and Deut. 18:15.
21. See Mark 8:31-33; Matt. 16:21-23; Luke 9:43-45.

22. J. Jeremias, *The Parables of Jesus,* rev. ed. (London: SCM, 1963), especially pp. 23-114.
23. Jeremias, *Parables,* p. 67.
24. A. Schweitzer, *The Quest of the Historical Jesus* (New York: Macmillan, 1968), p. 353.
25. Schweitzer, *Quest,* pp. 352-354.
26. For details see Joseph Klausner, *Jesus of Nazareth* (New York: Macmillan, 1925), p. 310.
27. B.Pes. 110a.
28. Schweitzer, *Quest,* pp. 393-394, 340.
29. Ibid., p. 393.
30. See J. Klausner, *Jesus,* pp. 342f.
31. Tosephta Kelim, B.Kam. 1:6, and b.Ket. 104a.
32. See, for example, B. J. Schniewind, *Das Evangelium nach Markus* (Göttingen, 1949), p. 121.
33. R. Bultmann, *Primitive Christianity in Its Contemporary Setting* (New York: Meridian Books, 1956), p. 92.
34. W. G. Kümmel *Promise and Fulfillment* (Naperville, Ill.: Allenson, 1957), p. 149.
35. K. Rahner and W. Thüsing, *Christologie—systematisch und exegetisch* (Freiburg, 1972), p. 28.
36. Hans Küng, *On Being a Christian* (Garden City, N.Y.: Doubleday, 1976), p. 167.
37. E. Schweizer, *Jesus,* pp. 13-14.
38. E. Käsemann, "The Problem of the Historical Jesus," in *Essays on New Testament Themes* (Naperville, Ill.: Allenson), p. 43.
39. F. Mussner, "Ursprünge und Entfaltung der ntl. Sohneschristologie," in *Grundfragen der Christologie heute* (Freiburg, 1975), pp. 88f.
40. M. Barth, "Was kann ein Jude von Jesus glauben und dennoch Jude bleiben," lecture held on 24 February 1965 in the Tree of Life Synagogue, Pittsburgh, published in Newsletter No. 2 of the Committee on the Church and the Jewish People of the World Council of Churches, Geneva, May 1965, pp. 6f.
41. B.Sanh. 97b.
42. J. Moltmann, *The Church in the Power of the Spirit* (New York: Harper and Row, 1977), p. 139.

Thesis Two: The people of Israel did not reject Jesus

1. So, for example, John 1:11 on p. 147; Matt. 13:13 on p. 37; Rom. 11:11 on p. 285; and Rom. 11:16 on p. 285.

2. Charlotte Klein, *Anti-Judaism in Christian Theology* (Philadelphia: Fortress, 1978), pp. 39-66.
3. *Tractatus adversus judaeos* 5-10, *P.L.* 42, pp. 54ff.
4. E. A. Synan, *The Popes and the Jews in the Middle Ages* (New York: Macmillan, 1965), pp. 37f.
5. *VI homilia adversus judaeos.*
6. AAS 40 (1948): 342.
7. *Missale romanum, editio Typica* (Vatican, 1970), p. 254.
8. M. Barth, *Jesus the Jew* (Atlanta: John Knox, 1978), pp. 21-22.
9. J. M. Robinson, in the introduction to A. Schweitzer, *The Quest of the Historical Jesus* (New York: Macmillan, 1968), pp. xiv-xv.
10. Th. Calmes, *L'evangile selon St. Jean* (Paris, 1904), pp. 60ff.
11. E. Grässer, "Die Juden als Teufelssöhne in Joh 8, 37-47," in *Antijudaismus im NT?* (Munich, 1967), p. 168.
12. C. Thoma, *Kirche aus Juden und Heiden* (Vienna, 1970), p. 89.
13. Demonstrated by Thoma, *Kirche,* p. 85; K. G. Echart, "Der zweite echte Brief des Apostels Paul an die Thessalonicher," *ZTK* 58 (1961): 33-34; G. S. Sloyan, *Jesus on Trial* (Philadelphia: Fortress, 1973), pp. 4f.
14. Origin, *Commentary* on Matt. 27:25.
15. Quoted by R. Pfisterer, *Im Schatten des Kreuzes* (Hamburg, 1966), p. 140.
16. J. Blinzer, *The Trial of Jesus* (Westminster, Md.: Newman, 1959), p. 290.
17. R. Guardini, *Der Herr,* 13th ed. (Würzburg, 1964), p. 109.
18. Michael Schmaus, *Katholische Dogmatik,* vol. II.2 (Munich, 1963), p. 124; see also M. Schmaus, *Dogma,* 5 vols (New York: Sheed and Sheed, 1968-1975), 3:92.
19. Schmaus, *Dogmatik,* p. 167.
20. E. Stauffer, *Jesus and His Story* (New York: Knopf, 1960), p. 131.
21. A. Schlatter, *Die Geschichte des Christus* (Stuttgart, 1921), p. 506 (reprinted 1977).
22. C. Thoma, *Kirche,* p. 90.
23. For details see Paul Winter, *On the Trial of Jesus* (Berlin: de Gruyter, 1961).
24. The Ethiopian church still celebrates June 25 as St. Pilate's Day.
25. The expression *deicidium* was coined in the year 165 by Melito, Bishop of Sardis, in his Passion Homilies.
26. I will pursue this issue in more detail elsewhere.
27. J.-F. Konrad, "Mitschuld durch Verkündigung," *ZRP* 3 (1977): 72.
28. W. Zimmerli, "Die Schuld am Kreuz," in *Israel und die Christen* (Neukirchen, 1964), pp. 24f.

29. C. Thoma, *Kirche,* p. 100.
30. *Christen und Juden—Eine Studie des Rates der Evangelischen Kirche in Deutschland* (Gutersloh, 1975), pp. 19, 22.

Thesis Three: Jesus never repudiated his people

1. Chrysostom, *Adv. Jud.* 2:3; 6:1.
2. References in *Revue des Études Juives* 11 (1972): 12.
3. References in *Kirche und Synagogue,* vol. 1 (Stuttgart, 1968), esp. pp. 30ff., 72, 85ff., 90-99; also in R. Pfisterer, *Im Schatten des Kreuzes* (Hamburg, 1966), pp. 38-46.
4. See, for example, Ezek. 16:59-62; Isa. 49:16; 61:8; Ps. 111:9; 1 Chron. 16:15ff.
5. H. Schlier, *Die Zeit der Kirche* (Freiburg, 1972), p. 242.
6. M. Schmaus, *Katholische Dogmatik,* vol. 4.2. (Munich, 1963), p. 167.
7. G. Schiwy, *Weg ins NT,* vol. 1 (Würzburg, 1970), p. 162.
8. These and other passages in Charlotte Klein, *Anti-Judaism in Christian Theology* (Philadelphia: Fortress, 1978), pp. 92-124.
9. J. Klausner, *Jesus of Nazareth* (New York: Macmillan, 1925), p. 375.
10. H. Küng, *On Being a Christian* (Garden City, N.Y.: Doubleday, 1976), p. 167.
11. Klausner, *Jesus,* pp. 389, 414.
12. P.Ber. 9,14b and p.Sota 5, 20c. The Talmud is a Jewish collection of rules and commandments for all situations of life, but it also contains biblical interpretations, wisdom sayings, anecdotes, and scholarly treatises.
13. J. Jeremias, *The Parables of Jesus,* rev. ed. (London: SCM, 1963), p. 18.
14. Ibid., p. 12.
15. Ibid., pp. 12f.
16. Ibid., p. 25.
17. Ibid., p. 29.
18. Ibid., p. 40.
19. Ibid., p. 94.
20. Ibid., p. 99.
21. Ibid., p. 108.
22. L. Goppelt, *Jesus, Paul and Judaism* (New York: Nelson, 1964), p. 93.
23. The *Jerusalem Bible* (Garden City, N.Y.: Doubleday, 1966), p. 49.
24. J. Schmid, *Das Evangelium nach Matthäus* (Regensburg, 1956), pp. 306f.
25. W. Trilling, *The Gospel according to St. Matthew* (New York: Herder and Herder, 1969), p. 151.
26. F. Mussner, "Die bösen Winzer nach Mt. 21, 33-46," in *Antijudaismus im NT?* (Munich, 1967), p. 129.

27. W. Trilling, *Das wahre Israel—Studien zur Theologie des Matthäus-Evangelium* (Munich, 1964), p. 16.
28. Jeremias, *Parables,* p. 72.
29. See, for example, Isa. 27:2-6; Jer. 12:10; Ps. 80:9-18.
30. F. Mussner, "Die bösen Winzer," p. 133.
31. Jeremias, *Parables,* pp. 70f., 74.
32. Ibid., p.73.
33. Ibid.
34. Ibid., pp. 74, 76.
35. According to codex Bezae and others.
36. The Hebrew collection of oral traditions; for the most part the Mishnah contains sayings of Jewish scribes in the first and second centuries A.D.
37. L. Baeck, *Paulus, Die Pharisäer und das NT* (Frankfurt, 1969), pp. 153f.
38. Compare Targum Jerus. on Exod. 15:12 and also B. Jakob, *Genesis* (Berlin, 1934), pp. 226, 248ff.
39. See Martin Hengel, *Die Zeloten* (Leiden, 1976), pp. 344f., 384ff.; and also Hengel, *Was Jesus a Revolutionist?* (Philadelphia: Fortress, 1971), pp. 21-35.
40. *The Fathers according to Rabbi Nathan* (Version B), trans. A. J. Saldarini (Leiden: E. J. Brill, 1975) 2:31 (p. 182).

Prolog for tomorrow

1. F. Rosenzweig, *Briefe* (Berlin, 1935), pp. 685ff.
2. Moses Maimonides, *Führer der Schwankenden,* 3:32.
3. H.-W. Bartsch, "Umkehr zu Israel," *Evangelische Zeitstimmen* 22/23 (Hamburg, 1965): 7f.

Part Two
A Christian Perspective by Ulrich Luz

Response to Thesis One

1. *Christ:* In the sayings of Jesus this title occurs only in Mark 12:35, in a general messianic discussion; in Mark 13:21, in relation to false Messiahs; and in Mark 9:41 (more than likely secondary to Matt. 10:42); and Matt. 23:10. All these are most likely community formulations. *Son of David:* In Jesus' words this title occurs only in Mark 12:35ff. (see above). *Son of God* (as distinguished from the absolute "the Son") never occurs in Jesus' words, but is particularly important in Christological legends (in both the baptism and transfiguration accounts in the speech

of God), in sayings addressed to demons (for example, Mark 3:11; 5:7), and in community confessions (for example, Matt. 14:33; 16:16; Mark 15:39). The Gospel of John has not been considered as a source for Jesus' sayings in this overview, nor will it be in my reply as a whole.

2. The Jews would have spoken of themselves as "Israel." The way Christians would have formulated it is shown by the Christologically influenced report of the trial, e.g., Mark 14:61; compare the mocking of the soldiers (Mark 15:18).

Response to Thesis Two

3. "Four years before the war . . . there came to the feast . . . one Jesus, son of Ananias, a rude peasant, who, standing in the temple, suddenly began to cry out, 'A voice from the east, a voice from the west, a voice from the four winds; a voice against Jerusalem and the sanctuary, a voice against the bridegroom and the bride, a voice against all the people.' . . . Some of the leading citizens . . . arrested the fellow and severely chastized him. But he, without a word on his own behalf . . . only continued his cries as before. Thereupon, the magistrates . . . brought him before the Roman governor; there, although flayed to the bone with scourges, he neither sued for mercy nor shed a tear, but . . . unceasingly reiterated his dirge over the city, until Albinus pronounced him a maniac and let him go" (Josephus, *War* 6.300-305 [trans. H. St. J. Thackeray; Loeb Classical Library; Harvard University Press, 1928]).
4. An exception: Matt. 27:62, a late editorial addition.
5. H. Frankemölle, *Jahwebund und Kirche Christi* (Münster, 1974), p. 306.
6. Why was R. Akiba, who solemnly proclaimed Simeon b. Kochba the Messiah, still considered orthodox? His execution by the Romans, to which he resigned himself completely, was even placed on the Day of Atonement (Midr. Prov. 9:2-31b)—presumably because it had an expiatory function for the people. By contrast, the transmitters of the "Sayings Source" were persecuted, even though they kept the law, because they awaited Jesus as the Son of man and judge of the world (see Luke 16:17; Matt. 23:23). James, the brother of Jesus, was unlawfully condemned by the high priest and punished by the Romans because he confessed Jesus as the "door" (Hegesippus 5 = Eusebius, *H.E.* 2:23.12ff.).
7. Apart from the Old Testament and Jewish reports of resurrection stories (see. P. Lapide, *The Resurrection of Jesus: A Jewish Perspective* [Minneapolis: Augsburg Publishing House, 1983], pp. 44-65), and apart from the possibilities that arise as a result of Old Testament accounts of the

translation of Enoch and Elijah, the following is particularly significant: The return of David or Hezekiah as the Messiah (Strack and Billerbeck, *Kommentar zum Neuen Testament aus Talmud und Midrasch,* 6 vols. [Munich, 1922-1961] 2:335-337). Since they, unlike Enoch, Elijah, Ezra, and Baruch (see 4 Ezra 14:9,49; 2 Bar. 13:3; 76:2), did not experience translation, their resurrection was presupposed. The basically Jewish tradition of the death, resurrection, and exaltation of the two witnesses (Rev. 11:3ff.) should also be kept in mind.

8. See Acts 6:14; 15:5f.; Gal. 2:3-5. Nevertheless, one ought not too quickly assume that the question of the Torah was the sole reason for the break between Christianity and Judaism; b.Yeb. 46a and the position of R. Jehoshua b. Hananiah show that at the time the possibility of abandoning circumcision itself, even apart from life-threatening circumstances, was discussed as an option for proselytes.
9. For evidence see the chapter on Paul in R. Smend, and U. Luz, in *Gesetz* (Stuttgart: Kohlhammer, 1981), pp. 89-112.
10. An impressive example is the statement of K. Barth about Israel, portraying the judgment of God on his congregation *(Church Dogmatics* 2.2., pp. 195-205).

Response to Thesis Three

11. Compare this with the 11th and 12th petitions of the "Eighteen Benedictions."
12. J. Klausner, *Jesus of Nazareth* (New York: Macmillan, 1925), pp. 370-377.
13. In addition to Mark 14:58 pars. and Mark 13:2, John 2:19-22 and Acts 6:14 should be considered. In these passages the word is not described as false witness.
14. I have in mind the author of the Temple Scroll of Qumran who places his own instructions beside the written Torah as the binding word of God. Whether it really was the teacher of righteousness who wrote the Temple Scroll is not important here.